Sport And Spirituality:

An Exercise In Everyday

Theology

D1518167

edited by Gordon Preece and Rob Hess

ATF Press
Adelaide

Interface: A Forum for Theology in the World

Volume 11 Number 1

Interface is an ecumenical and interdisciplinary theological journal
dealing with issues of a social and cultural nature.
Interface is an independently refereed journal and listed on the list of
the DEST Register of Refereed journals.
Editorial Board
Editor in Chief: Rev Dr Gordon Watson, Port Macquarie, New South
Wales
Chairman: Rev Dr David Rankin, Trinity Theological College, Brisbane
Dr Elizabeth Hepburn IBVM, St Mary's College, Melbourne
Dr Anne Hunt, Australian Catholic University, Ballarat
Dr Winifred Wing Han Lamb, Australian National University,
Canberra
Revd Dr James McEvoy Catholic Theological College, Flinders
University / Adelaide College of Divinity, Adelaide
Revd Dr Denis Minns OP, Catholic Institute of Sydney
Revd Dr Vic Pfitzner, Adelaide, South Australia
Mr Hilary Regan, ATF Executive Officer, Adelaide

Mailing address:
Interface, PO Box 504, Hindmarsh, SA 5007
email: hdregan@atf.org.au
ATF Home Page: www.atf.org.au

Subscription Rates
Australia: Individual and institutions Aus $52 p/a (includes GST)
Overseas: Individual and institutions Aus $60 p/a
Send all subscriptions to:
Interface
PO Box 504
Hindmarsh SA 5007

Interface is published by the Australasian Theological Forum Ltd
(ABN 90 116 359 963) and is published in May and October of each year.
Interface is indexed in the *Australasian Religion Index*
ISSN 1329-6264

Sport And Spirituality: An Exercise In Everyday Theology

Contents

Editorial

Gordon Preece and Rob Hess

The intersection between sport and spirituality has attracted unprecedented academic interest in the first decade of the twenty-first century, as a general survey of the field in this volume by Rob Hess shows. One sign of a quickening of interest in the area has been the emergence of academic conferences devoted to the theme, with one (held in the United States in 2004) generating considerable interest among the sport history community, and another (held in Great Britain in 2007) providing the impetus for the establishment of the *International Journal of Religion and Sport*. Other beacons have been tertiary courses devoted to the field, notably a new unit 'Sport and Spirituality' taught by former Olympian Richard Pengelly at the University of Western Australia, and the newly established Centre for the Study of Sport and Spirituality at York St John University in England.[1]

Alongside these developments has been a steady stream of related academic publications, reflective of the growing general interest in the discipline of sports studies.[2] While a detailed literature review is not the intention of this introduction, a listing of several pertinent books gives an indication of how publications in the field have flowered in recent times. A small chronological selection from the last decade and a half reveals such works as the collection by Hoffman, *Sport and Religion*,[3] the national study by Higgs, *God in the Stadium: Sports and Religion in America*,[4]

---

1. See, respectively, Brendan O'Keefe, 'UWA Resurrects Sport's Spiritual Parallels', *Australian*, 8 November 2006, 25, and http://sportspirituality.yorksj.ac.uk
2. The academic study of sport history, in particular, is a burgeoning field, with societies existing in North America, Britain and Australia, as well as other places in the world. The first such society was the North American Society for Sport History, which was formed in 1973. For a recent overview of the field, see Martin Johnes, 'Putting the History into Sport: On Sport History and Sports Studies in the UK', *Journal of Sport History*, vol. 31, no. 2 (Summer 2004), 145-160.
3. Shirl J. Hoffman, editor, *Sport and Religion* (Champaign: Illinois, 1992).
4. Robert J. Higgs, *God in the Stadium: Sports and Religion in America* (Lexington:

Magdalinski and Chandler's international anthology, *With God on Their Side: Sport in the Service of Religion*,[5] and Baker's substantive *Playing with God: Religion and Modern Sport*.[6] Most recent of all is *Sport and Spirituality*, a publication instigated by key players in the international conference of the same name.[7] While the majority of these titles have their basis in the social sciences, particularly history and social psychology, none have the concentrated theological focus of the articles contained in this issue.

The essays then move in a more specifically Christian direction with Gordon Preece's preview of what a Protestant play ethic might look like. Vic Pfitzner's enlightening survey of ancient and biblical athletic imagery maintains the strong theological and Christian focus. As does Synthia Sydnor's robust apologia of a distinctively Catholic view of the body, femininity and sport. Richard Hutch's 'Sport, Sailing and Human Spirituality' illustrates one of the perils or perhaps potentials of a venture such as this journal. Authors can operate with quite different definitions of spirituality. Hutch elects to go with William James' definition of spirituality as what individuals do with their solitude with the divine. Others, one editor (Preece) included, would have a more corporate definition of spirituality. The editors chose not to be definitive or prescriptive to the authors at this point.

In attempting to outline 'A Protestant Play Ethic', Gordon Preece bounces off Eric Liddell's remark to his spiritually concerned sister Jenny in the 1981 Oscar-winning film *Chariots of Fire*. Liddell eases her worries concerning his vocation to the mission field, but only after he runs in the Olympics. He says: 'God made me *fast* Jenny, and when I run, I feel God's pleasure'. The alleged clash between Jenny and Eric Liddell is emblematic of that between those who see sport as either unspiritual or redeemable as a utilitarian means to spiritual ends for

University Press of Kentucky, 1995).

5.   Tara Magdalinski and T. J. L. Chandler, editors, *With God on Their Side: Sport in the Service of Religion* (London: Routledge, 2002).

6.   William J. Baker, *Playing with God: Religion and Modern Sport* (Cambridge: Harvard University Press, 2007). See also his earlier lecture series, William J. Baker, *If Christ Came to the Olympics* (Sydney: University of New South Wales Press, 2000).

7.   Jim Parry, Simon Robinson, Nick J. Watson and Mark Nesti, editors, *Sport and Spirituality: An Introduction* (London: Routledge, 2007).

example evangelism (Jenny) and those who see sport as an expression of spirituality, as intrinsically good in God's eyes.

Preece uses Eric Liddell's comment as a stimulus toward a long-overdue Protestant Play Ethic. He first sets play in the context of a theology of divine and human pleasure. Then he narrates certain forms of play as pleasurable ends in themselves, firstly the personal, female story of Stephanie Paulsell's running and then the more corporate one of Credo Cricket, critiquing various utilitarian perversions of play as mere means to an end.

Victor C Pfitzner's essay is entitled 'We are the Champions! Origins and Developments of the Image of God's Athletes'. He notes:

> That games and gods belonged together was taken for granted in the ancient world, whether at the classical Greek athletic contests of Olympia, Nemea, Pythia or Isthmia, at the dramatic contests in Athens, or at the more bellicose and brutal gladiatorial games of the Romans. Contests between the gods belong to the oldest myths of Greek literature, so it is not surprising that the origins and ideals of the great national contests were found in the myths of gods and heroes.

The great fifth century BCE tragedians and philosophers laid claim to greater strength and skill than the athletes though.

However, ancient Hebrew contains no words for athletic games. It is in the intersection between Hebraic and Hellenistic culture that the use of athletic imagery comes to the fore in Judeo-Christian contexts. The Maccabean martyrs are portrayed in such terms in their contest against the Hellenists. Philo portrays Moses, Joseph, Enoch, Noah, and even the wandering Israelites as God's athletic champions competing against human passions, not for personal but divine glory. Athletic imagery is baptized by the apostle Paul, speaking of himself and his co-workers in such terms in 1 Cor 9:24–27 among other passages. The book of Hebrews portrays the Christian martyr athlete. Stoic sages, Maccabean martyrs, Christian apostles compete as much with internal as external opponents. Pfitzner concludes by arguing for the positive use of sporting imagery as far preferable to the use of militaristic imagery today.

Synthia Sydnor's essay sets issues related to sport and femininity in terms of Christian, and specifically Catholic thought. She has two purposes: First, to outline a rationale for taking such a topic seriously in contrast to how academia and journalism in the past two decades regarding 'femininity and sport' has rarely included a Christian reading of these issues; Second, she testifies to becoming a Catholic and researching Pope John Paul II's 'theology of the body' as a new kind of feminism in Christ applicable to the study of sport.

This 'new feminism' of John Paul II, identifies the male 'debt' owed to women, who sacrifice 'for the bearing of life' (Leonie Caldercott) as a key concept liberating to culture. In usual studies concerning femininity and sport, the paradigm of liberation, of openness, is dominant. Why not, Sydnor suggests, put this in dialogue with John Paul II's conception of a human rational and wisdom-based culture forming an 'organic whole with nature'. In predominantly secular American sport sociology, it has been too long taboo to dialogue with such an alternative philosophy and phenomenology of bodily movement, play and competition. This papal perspective challenges the exoticizing and making definitive of particular sub-cultures and practices of women in sport in third wave feminist ethnography.

John Paul II's body theology challenges the dominant monologue on gender and sport studies because it asserts that the body reveals God, it is a gift from God. Because feminine nature privileges women's distinct physical and spiritual capabilities for participating in the social order, modern dualism about women in sport is rejected in his theology of the body. Sydnor's use of John Paul II's theology of the body has interesting links with Preece's use of Paulsell's Christian feminist account of her rediscovery of bodily joy in running through the complimentarity of running with her husband after losing that joy in the heat of adolescent angst and male-female antagonism.

Richard Hutch illustrates James' famous individualistic definition of spirituality which certainly fits his subject matter – that of lone, round-the-world-yachtsmen and women. Drawing on accounts from their journals, logs and interviews, Hutch highlights the tensions in the experience of such sailors: between self-confidence and awe before the ocean's power; between self-reliance and divine dependence. He sees solo sailing the globe as a microcosm of human smallness before the vastness of the universe which the Copernican Revolution opened up beyond the anthropocentric Ptolemaic universe. Facing death in the ocean's open jaws is a salutary spiritual experience as are the 'interruptions to utopian aspirations and heightened positive aesthetic experiences individuals may enjoy at sea. The argument of this paper is that such interruptions can give rise to new moral postures toward living. These postures represent invigorated spiritual meaning and purpose…'

Chris Gardiner's 'The Call of the Game' is written by a 'reflective practitioner'. He is CEO of Police & Community Youth Clubs NSW, and a football (soccer) referee and club president. His essay is his way of 'reflecting on how humans experience and build value through the rule-based activities called games, reflect on how important referees are to experiencing the value we seek, and think[ing] about the virtues that might be articulated to underpin the practice and service of the referee'. In this he draws on the ground-breaking work of Alisdair MacIntyre on how social practices shape virtues and our humanity.

Gardiner puts this personally and passionately: 'like so many others, football matters to me—I love the game, it adds to my identity, it helps me explain what it means to be human—to my children, to my friends, to my community'. While Gardiner's paper has little overt vertical spirituality of sport, it eloquently gives voice to its horizontal, human, communal aspect. However, for this to be maintained, for the game to 'flow', and for humans to flourish in their practice of it, rules and referees are required. His basic point is that 'many of us respond to the "call of the game", but whether we actually enjoy the resulting experience depends on the referee's actual call of the game, and that, therefore, we should do more to ensure that that call is consistently excellent'. That sense of 'flow', of excellent, energetic humanity, flourishing in sport, may even echo a higher call, a divine pleasure in sweaty, spiritual sport, something Eric Liddell felt in his feet.

Chapter One

Sphere Of Sweat: Sport, History And Spirituality

Rob Hess

Intersections between sport and religion have attracted unprecedented academic interest in the last decade and a half. This article explores the evidence for this quickening, drawing largely on published material from the field of the social sciences (rather than theological literature), to track developments in the area. The discipline of sport history is used as a case study, not only because scholars in this province have been at the forefront of exploring such intersections, but also because prominent sport historians have openly challenged the academic credibility of these studies. For this reason, some general background on the emergence of sport history as an academic discipline is provided, and then two inter-connected aspects related to the recent upsurge in sport and spirituality are discussed in turn, namely academic literature, and academic conferences and course work. A brief summary is offered by way of a conclusion.

Background: the rise of sport history

The growth of sport, particularly in its modern and now postmodern forms, has been widely acknowledged as an unparalleled social phenomenon.[1] It is not surprising, therefore, that sport has come under significant scrutiny by academics. In the English-speaking world, the beginnings of this analysis can be traced back to the physical education profession of the 1930s. According to Jack Berryman, it was Seward

The author wishes to acknowledge advice from Gordon Preece (Urban Seed) and Matthew Klugman (Victoria University) during the preparation of this article.

1. For the most comprehensive, single-volume history of sport, see Allen Guttmann, *Sports: The First Five Millenia* (Amherst: University of Massachusetts Press, 2004).

Stanley, a professor of physical education at the University of Illinois, who first urged that courses in the history of sport should be part of a physical education student's professional training, and from 1937, with few exceptions, it was those physical educators who initially provided the impetus for the scholarly study of sport history.[2] But these practitioners were trained in physical education, not history. As a general rule, their desire was to understand the emergence of educational attitudes towards physical activity, and then explore the social ramifications of sport itself. They were gatherers of information, and their training did not reflect formal historical practices. They undertook sport history, as Don Morrow explains, because professionally trained historians, for whatever reason, had chosen not to investigate the subject area.[3]

By the early 1950s, the study of sport still wandered in the 'intellectual badlands'. As Paul Zingg notes, 'Ignored by scholars who stuck to traditional modes of inquiry in their disciplines and impaired by efforts which reflected naivety and simplicity, sport history studies generally provided few contributions to understanding ... culture and society'.[4] All that physical educators (and most journalists, for that matter) produced during this period was a stream of books that were '. . . embarrassingly hagiographic, tediously statistical, and remarkable superficial'.[5] In short, the material lacked methodological substance and analytical depth.[6]

2.   JW Berryman, 'Sport History as Social History?', *Quest*, XX (June 1973), 66.

3.   Don Morrow, 'Canadian Sport History: A Critical Essay', *Journal of Sport History*, 10/1 (1983), 73. Perhaps the most influential work of sport history that emerged from the 1930s was EN Gardiner, *Athletics of the Ancient World* (Oxford: Clarendon Press, 1930). For a critical commentary on Gardiner's often reprinted seminal work, see DG Kyle, 'E Norman Gardiner: Historian of Ancient Sport', *International Journal of the History of Sport*, 8/1 (May 1991), 28–55.

4.   PJ Zingg, 'Introduction', *The Sporting Image: Readings in American Sport History*, edited by PJ Zingg (Lanham, MD: University Press of America, 1988), ix.

5.   *Ibid.* Guttmann calls both physical educators and journalists 'amateur' historians, claiming they have traditionally been uncritical and inaccurate in their sport histories. Allen Guttmann, *A Whole New Ball Game: An Interpretation of American Sports* (Chapel Hill: University of North Carolina Press, 1988), 212.

6.   Two notable exceptions from the middle decades of the century, both of which broadened the paradigm of sports studies by their philosophical consideration of play and leisure, were not originally published in English. See Johan Huizinga, *Homo Ludens: A Study of the Play Element in Culture* (London: Routledge and Kegan Paul, 1949 [Originally published in 1938]), and Josef Pieper, *Leisure: The Basis of*

However, the situation began to change as the political ferment of the 1960s led to new intellectual attitudes. The shallowness, elitism and inadequacy that frequently characterized conservative interpretations of society began to be challenged, and these challenges opened the door for fresh inquiries in the fields of social history and popular culture. Social history, in particular, increasingly came to be seen by its adherents as a total historical approach, with sport studies as part of that overall perspective.[7] By the 1970s, a number of scholars with social history backgrounds began to determine the agenda and direction of sport history. As Nancy Struna has observed:

> These historians avoided the presentist, institutional, and almost prescriptive qualities, as well as the narrow and inappropriate evidential bases, which had prevailed in the research; and in a more nearly adequate manner and in terms of the subjects, they uncovered and transmitted 'the experiences of the people' of the past.[8]

Even so, despite the fact that the baton of sports studies scholarship had passed from physical educators to social historians, very few of the latter appeared to recognize the potential of sport as a heuristic device. Indeed, the study of sport was still seen as rather peripheral and unlikely to contribute anything of value to what was perceived as 'real' history.[9] Moreover, in the view of some trenchant critics, there

---

Culture (London: Pantheon Books, 1952 [Originally published in 1947]).

7.   The term social history was initially used in reference to the poor or lower classes. See EJ Hobsbawm, 'From Social History to the History of Society', *Daedalus*, 100 (Winter 1971), 21.

8.   NL Struna, 'In "Glorious Disarray": The Literature of American Sport History', *Research Quarterly for Exercise and Sport*, 56/2 (1985), 155.

9.   Richard Cashman, 'The Making of Sporting Traditions, 1977–87', *Australian Society for Sports History Bulletin*, 10 (December 1989), 15–16. For similar overviews of these and other relevant historiographical issues at the time, see Elizabeth Fox-Genovese and ED Genovese, 'The Political Crisis of Social History: A Marxian Perspective', *Journal of Social History*, 10/2 (Winter 1976), 205–20, and Gerald Redmond, 'Sport History in Academe: Reflections on a Half Century of Peculiar Progress', *British Journal of Sport History*, 1/1 (May 1984), 24–40. A special issue of the *Journal of Sport History* was also devoted to a review of the discipline. In particular, see Allen

were also fundamental flaws in the basic documents of sport history, for the source material was considered to be uneven and lacking sufficient depth for analysis, and there was no appropriate methodology to inform practitioners in the field.[10] Thus it can be understood why the early works of sports historians were often defensive in their outlook and tentative in their conclusions.

Nevertheless, it was not long before a number of academic societies devoted specifically to the history of sport were formed. While some of these organizations received their impetus from earlier gatherings of physical educators with a bent for history, it was perhaps inevitable that a growing number of social historians with a special interest in the history of sport began to dominate the field. The academic study of sport history blossomed in the 1970s and early 1980s, with societies established independently of each other in North America, Britain and Australia, as well as other places in the world.[11] Like most academic associations, these sport history societies continue to exist in order to 'promote, stimulate, and encourage study and research and writing' in their discipline.[12] To achieve their goals, the organizations concerned run conferences and publish journals, and, in the last decade, most have set up websites for the dissemination of information related to their activities. In the case of sport history, an international listserv ('Sporthist') also exists, with more

---

Guttmann, 'Recent Work in European Sports History', *Journal of Sport History*, 10/1 (Spring 1983), 35–52, and W. J. Baker, 'The State of British Sport History', *Journal of Sport History*, 10/1 (Spring 1983), 53–66.

10. Cashman, *op cit*, 16. For later comments on the problems associated with the nature of sports history documentation, see Richard Cox, 'A Model for Sports History Documentation: The Origins, Objectives, Methods, Findings and Recommendations of the British Sports History Bibliography Project', *International Journal of the History of Sport*, 9/2 (August 1992), 252–79.

11. The first such society was the North American Society for Sport History, which was formed in 1972. This was followed by the British Society for Sport History (1982) and the Australian Society for Sports History (1983). For recent critical overviews of the field, see Martin Johnes, 'Putting the History into Sport: On Sport History and Sports Studies in the UK', in *Journal of Sport History*, 31/2 (Summer 2004), 145–160, and Douglas Booth, *The Field: Truth and Fiction in Sport History* (London: Routledge, 2005).

12. See the North American Society for Sport History Mission Statement at http://nassh.org/index1.html, accessed 8 February 2008.

than 600 subscribers from around the world, although the great majority of these subscribers are based in tertiary institutions in North America.

Thus, from an uncertain beginning, the study of sport history has developed to a point where it may now be regarded as 'a respectable and growing enterprise', relatively well established in academe.[13] Historians of sport have begun to use a variety of data-gathering techniques to create significant new archives, which have superseded the more narrow sources of previous generations. It is no longer necessary to rely on shallow biographies or the back page panegyric of the press for suitable material, and the result is more informed, more penetrating, and more confident analyses of sport in a wider cultural context.[14] In addition, as David Vanderwerken notes, such developments have also assisted, and perhaps have also been assisted by, a concomitant growth in the teaching of sport studies in academic institutions. As he explains, 'It is a rare college or university catalog [*sic*] that does not have sport-related listings in its arts and sciences curricula'. He argues that sport studies are legitimate and that 'They have arrived'. Thus it is 'probably time to stop being apologetic and defensive'.[15] It is within this general historiographical setting that the literature dealing with specific aspects of sport and spirituality in an academic context can be discussed.

Sport and spirituality: academic literature

Entwined in the burgeoning field of sports studies literature, there is a small but steadily growing niche of material devoted to the general topic

---

13. Cashman, *op cit*, 25. Evidence for this view in the Australian context is reflected in the fact that regular conferences on 'Sporting Traditions' have been held since 1977, the Australian Society for Sports History was formed in 1983, and a specialist journal and bulletin have been published since 1984. Papers from the first two conferences were subsequently published. See *Sport in History*, edited by Richard Cashman and Michael McKernan (St Lucia: University of Queensland Press, 1979), and Richard Cashman and Michael McKernan, eds, *Sport: Money, Morality and the Media* (Sydney: University of New South Wales Press, 1981).

14. Cashman, *op cit*, 21.

15. DL Vanderwerken, 'By Way of Preface and Introduction: The Stabilizing of Sports Studies', in *Sport in the Classroom: Teaching Sport-Related Courses in the Humanities*, edited by DL Vanderwerken (Cranbury, NJ: Associated University Presses, 1990), 11. It should be noted that an increasing number of subjects and courses in the sports humanities are being offered at tertiary institutions throughout Australasia.

of sport and religion, along with the more recent off-shoot of sport and spirituality. A survey of international publications from the last decade and a half reveals several monographs, dozens of journal articles, and a number of anthologies. While an extensive and detailed review of the literature is not the intention of this section of the article, a brief discussion of three significant collected works provides both a handy overview of some of the pertinent themes and issues, and gives an indication of how, where and why such material is being generated. The three titles concerned include the 1992 collection by Shirl Hoffman, *Sport and Religion*,[16] Tara Magdalinski and Tim Chandler's 2002 international anthology, *With God on Their Side: Sport in the Service of Religion*,[17] and the compilation edited by Jim Parry, Simon Robinson, Nick Watson and Mark Nesti entitled *Sport and Spirituality*, published in 2007.[18] While these titles essentially have their basis in the social sciences, particularly history, sociology, philosophy and social psychology, none have a concentrated theological focus, and all emanate from the efforts of editors situated in tertiary academic settings.[19] In other words, these works demonstrate that there is a distinct genre of relevant writing that lies largely outside theological discourse, focusing as it does on the socio-cultural dimensions of sport.

In this context, Hoffman's anthology, comprised of 25 chapters, is quite insular, being primarily concerned with modern sport, and having a heavy emphasis on North American perspectives. The book is divided into four sections. As Hoffman explains, in the first part, 'Sport as Religion', definitions of religion are debated, and the notion that sport

16. See *Sport and Religion*, edited by SJ Hoffman (Champaign: Illinois, Human Kinetics, 1992).

17. See *With God on their Side: Sport in the Service of Religion*, edited by Tara Magdalinski and TJL Chandler (London: Routledge, 2002).

18. *Sport and Spirituality: An Introduction*, edited by Jim Parry, Simon Robinson, NJ Watson and Mark Nesti (London: Routledge, 2007).

19. See also *From Season to Season: Sports as American Religion*, edited by JL Price (Macon, GA: Mercer University Press, 2001), where the majority of chapters (most written by Price himself) are devoted to an analysis of American baseball, football, basketball, hockey and wrestling. Price is a professor of religious studies at Whittier College in the United States. Another relevant publication, with a heavy North American focus, is WJ Baker, *Playing with God: Religion and Modern Sport* (Cambridge: Harvard University Press, 2007).

somehow represents a new American religion is explored. In 'Sport as Religious Experience', the claim that sports lovers can discover religious meaning through sport is examined. Within the third section, 'Religion in Sport', the so-called 'religious trappings' of American sport are analysed, along with the problems concerning the 'sport-religion mix'. Finally, in 'Sport, Religion and Ethics', a variety of 'religion-based ethical positions' are considered. Although Hoffman acknowledges that the boundaries of religion were deliberately kept flexible, he acknowledges that in the book 'Christianity receives the lion's share of attention.'[20] Nearly all of the chapters have been reproduced from a range of earlier works, with the earliest, 'Sport: Morality and Ethics', dating from Howard Slusher's *Man, Sport and Existence*, published in 1967, and others derived from magazines such as *Sports Illustrated* and *New Catholic World*. Some of the material is populist in nature, but Hoffman's introductions to each of the four parts help to synthesize the literature and provide a context for the thematic selections. Overall, historical aspects are often assumed rather than specifically dealt with, as the contributors seek to explore the importance of both sport and religion to the social landscape. In effect, Hoffman's collection is representative of studies that use aspects of history as the basis for broadly sociological insights, and in this case there is a strong sense that the anthology is directed at the American tertiary college marketplace.[21]

---

20. SJ Hoffman, 'Preface', in *Sport and Religion,* edited by SJ Hoffman (Champaign: Illinois, 1992), vii–viii.

21. See also *Religion and Sport: The Meaning of Sacred and Profane,* edited by Charles Prebish (Westport, GT: Greenwood, 1993). Robert Higgs suggests that the anthologies by Hoffman and Prebish are complementary and 'would make excellent texts for much needed courses'. RJ Higgs, 'Review Essay', in *Journal of the Philosophy of Sport*, XXIII (1996), 108. In a lucid turn of phrase, Higgs declares that both books demonstrate the depth of interaction between 'a celestial sphere of metaphysics and the earthy sphere of sweat', 104. For other relevant works by Higgs himself, see RJ Higgs, *The Sporting Spirit: Athletes in Literature and Life* (New York: Harcourt Brace Jovanovich, 1977), and RJ Higgs, *God in the Stadium: Sports and Religion in America* (Lexington: University Press of Kentucky, 1995). Also worthy of note is RJ Higgs and MC Braswell, *An Unholy Alliance: The Sacred and Modern Sports* (Macon, GA: Mercer University Press, 2004). This latter publication offers a dissenting opinion to the increasingly persistent claim that sports are a form of religion. In particular, Higgs and Braswell challenge the use of ancient mythological parallels as a justification for viewing sport as religion.

In contrast, the compilation by Magdalinski and Chandler serves to broaden and stretch the existing intellectual paradigms with a series of explicit historical case studies that range not only in geographical coverage but in social and religious contexts. Thus, not only is sport and Christian fundamentalism considered, but also religion, race and rugby in South Africa, Shinto and sumo in Japan, and sport and Islam in France and North Africa, to name just some of the topics covered by contributors. Helpfully, Magdalinski and Chandler introduce their collection with a lengthy chapter of their own, whereby they survey the field and introduce the material of the contributors. In their view, an emphasis on whether or not sport should be conceived as a religion 'obscures the complexities of this relationship'.[22] For this reason, their volume deliberately sets out to 'investigate the role of sport and religion in the social formation of collective groups' and they are 'specifically concerned with the means by which sport might operate in the service of a religious community and assist in the promulgation of its theology'.[23] In essence, then, the focus in this anthology is on new work that considers the intersections of sport with organised religion, rather than work that is based around exploring the notion of sport as religion. Even more so than Hoffman, Magdalinski and Chandler's definition of what constitutes religion is specifically articulated. They do not regard religious behaviour 'as simply emblematic of an individual's own personal faith, nor as just an imposed power structure from an organised church'. Instead, they recognise that 'religion intersects both personal devotion and social and cultural institutions and has a significant impact on the formation of both the individual and group identities'.[24] It is notable, however, that while virtually all the chapters are underpinned by historical methodologies, the concept of 'spirituality' is not covered in any significant way, and discussion is limited largely to forms of organised religion.

If the three anthologies under consideration represent samples from a typology, then the title of the jointly edited work by Parry, Robinson, Watson and Nesti reflects an important aspect of academic focus and

---

22. Tara Magdalinski and TJL Chandler, 'With God on their Side: An Introduction', in, *With God on their Side: Sport in the Service of Religion,* edited by Tara Magdalinski and TJL Chandler (London: Routledge, 2002), 2.
23. *Ibid.*
24. *Ibid.*

deserves a somewhat more extended treatment. As the dust jacket proclaims, *Sport and Spirituality: An Introduction* explores elements of the sports experience through the perspectives of sport psychology, philosophy, ethics, theology and religious studies. In the Introduction, the editors posit that the idea of spirituality has 'begun to break loose from the meaning structures that held it together for centuries, not least the framework of formal religion'.[25] They acknowledge that 'there is no settled view of what spirituality is', hence the development of thematic schema for the book.[26] The anthology is divided into four sections, and in contrast to other works previously discussed, the entire first part of three chapters is set aside for an explicit discussion of 'Sport and Spirituality'. Indeed, Simon Robinson devotes sixteen pages to uncovering a working definition of 'spirituality', an indicator of how central this concept is to the overall content of the book.[27] In this section, the notion of a 'generic' view of spirituality is outlined, where 'life meaning' in the context of holistic and community perspectives is construed in various ways, and is related to sport in its widest sense and scope 'from the individual sportsperson's or team's experience to the organisation and management of sports institutions, and to the wider community of stakeholders in sport—media, spectators, fans and so on'.[28]

The second section is allocated to 'formal religions' and how these shed light on applied spirituality. Here, in a section with a strong historical focus, Watson contributes three chapters that deal with the 'win at all costs' attitude in modern sport, the historical and theological development of 'muscular Christianity' and the emergence of evangelical Protestant organisations and ministries in modern sport, and the nature of the mystical and the sublime as evident in the practice of extreme sports, which by definition may lead to injury or death.[29] In Watson's introduction to the section, he also makes the claim that theologians, by

25. Jim Parry, Simon Robinson, NJ Watson and Mark Nesti, 'Introduction', in *Sport and Spirituality: An Introduction*, edited by Jim Parry, Simon Robinson, NJ Watson and Mark Nesti (London: Routledge, 2007), 1.

26. *Ibid.*

27. Simon Robinson, 'Spirituality: A Working Definition', in *Sport and Spirituality: An Introduction*, edited by Jim Parry, Simon Robinson, NJ Watson and Mark Nesti (London: Routledge, 2007), 22–37.

28. Parry, Robinson, Watson and Nesti, 'Introduction', *op cit*, 1–2.

29. The first of the three chapters in this section is co-written with John White.

Rob Hess

and large, have been reluctant to reflect seriously on sport, despite its predominance as a 'cultural pastime'.[30]

Mark Nesti, a sport psychologist, follows the pattern of the book by then offering a section consisting of a triptych of chapters on the topic of 'Existential Psychology and Sport'. He attempts to show how the discipline of sport psychology should consider the spiritual dimensions of sport, with the aim of developing 'an acceptance of the idea of a person as an embodied spiritual being'.[31] This section flows naturally from Watson's aforementioned discussion of the mystical in sport, and is reminiscent, though far more advanced, than previous works from the 1970s on the psychic dimensions of physical activity.[32] However, the editors are candid in noting that although psychology can provide useful insights into personal and social identity and experience, especially in the relationship between therapy and sport, there are 'many questions from different schools of psychology that contest these approaches, fuelling ongoing debates'.[33]

The final section in the anthology again consists of three chapters, but the focus is on 'Ethics, Olympism and Spirituality'. Religiosity has always been associated with the Olympic Games, and the general literature on this topic is very extensive.[34] In this section of the book, the

30. Jim Parry, Simon Robinson, NJ Watson and Mark Nesti, 'Religion and Sport', in *Sport and Spirituality: An Introduction*, edited by Jim Parry, Simon Robinson, NJ Watson and Mark Nesti (London: Routledge, 2007), 59. Note: each of the sections is preceded by an overview, presumably jointly written by the editors of the book.

31. Jim Parry, Simon Robinson, NJ Watson and Mark Nesti, 'Existential Psychology and Sport', in *Sport and Spirituality: An Introduction*, edited by Jim Parry, Simon Robinson, NJ Watson and Mark Nesti (London: Routledge, 2007), 117.

32. See, for example, Michael Murphy and RA White, *The Psychic Side of Sports* (Reading, MA: Addison-Wesley, 1978). For a recent, more extended treatment of existentialism and the psychoanalytical aspects of a particular set of sporting experiences, see Richard Hutch, *Lone Sailors and Spiritual Insights: Cases of Sport and Peril at Sea* (Lewiston, NY: Edwin Mellen Press, 2005).

33. Parry, Robinson, Watson and Nesti, 'Introduction', *op cit*, 2.

34. See, for example, G Papantoniou, 'Religiosity as a Main Element in the Ancient Olympic Games', in *Sport in Society*, 11/1 (January 2008), 32–43, JJ MacAloon, 'Religious Themes and Structures in the Olympic Movement and the Olympic Games', in *Philosophy, Theology and History of Sport and of Physical Education*, edited by Fernand Landry and WAR Orban (Miami: Symposia Specialists, 1978), 161-69, and WJ Baker, *If Christ Came to the Olympics* (Sydney: University of New South

discussion is obviously more philosophical in nature, and connections between virtues, moral education, rule structures, and the ethos of sport are examined. The ideology of Olympism is explored in detail, and the final chapter is devoted to the place of religious sentiment in ancient and modern sport. In summing up this material, Jim Parry expresses the over-arching view that: 'Sport is thus seen as a spiritual practising of our ethical and political values—as an embodiment and expression of holistic and value-based meaning, expressing a sense of value and purpose in relation to ourselves and others'.[35]

In summing up, it is also worth noting that *Sport and Spirituality: An Introduction* is explicitly designed as a text book, with study questions listed at the end of each chapter. Moreover, Parry and Robinson are academics at tertiary institutions in Leeds, while Watson and Nesti are both sport psychologists at York St John University, so their anthology is partly a response to developments that are dealt with in brief below, namely the advent of academic conferences and academic courses related to sport and spirituality.

Sport and spirituality: academic conferences and course work

As mentioned previously, sport historians from around the world use a listserv, 'Sporthist', to post fairly benign research inquiries, to provide historical commentary on contemporary sports news, or to advise subscribers of forthcoming events or conferences. On 2 January 2004, Gary Wicks sent a post to the listserv, announcing 'an upcoming conference on religion and sport'.[36] He provided a link to a website address, confirmed that the conference was to be held at St Olaf's College in the United States, and encouraged the submission of proposals for papers. Wicks

---

Wales Press, 2000).

35. Jim Parry, Simon Robinson, NJ Watson and Mark Nesti, 'Ethics, Olympism and Spirituality', in *Sport and Spirituality: An Introduction,* edited by Jim Parry, Simon Robinson, N.J Watson and Mark Nesti (London: Routledge, 2007), 171. It should be noted that the philosophy of sport is a well established field. Sport philosophers have their own academic society and a dedicated journal that has been published by Human Kinetics since 1974. For details of the International Association for the Philosophy of Sport, see http://iaps.glos.ac.uk/index.html.

36. The Sporthist list is archived at: http://listserv.manchester.ac.uk/archives/sporthist.html. Emails referred to in this article can be accessed at this site.

concluded his email by asking subscribers 'to consider joining us for
excellent dialog [*sic*] and discussion on this significant topic'. His posting
generated a flurry of email responses, and the wide array of rejoinders
is instructive for examining a number of issues related to the juncture of
sport, history and spirituality.

The first response to the Wicks email came from Andrew Ritchie, a
cycling historian and regular contributor to 'Sporthist'. Ritchie and a
number of other sport historians, notably Dorothy Jane Mills, queried
the relevance of the conference, the narrow mission statement of St Olaf's
College (an affiliate of the Evangelical Lutheran Church of America), and
wondered, for example, whether delegates would be called upon to pray
at the conference. Others such as Annmarie Jutel feared that Christian
perspectives would outweigh any other faiths that were represented
at the gathering, with Ritchie challenging Wicks as to whether it was
appropriate to stage an academic conference on religion and sport at
an avowedly Christian college. The electronic debate raged for almost
two weeks as battle lines were quickly drawn between secularists and
those more open to the discussion of spiritual concerns in an academic
context. Synthia Sydnor, Darcy Plymire, Rusty Wilson, and Karen Fox
were among those who defended the relevance and credibility of the
proposed conference. The conference eventually took place in June 2004,
but some of the issues raised by members of 'Sporthist' continued to
simmer. These matters also became enmeshed in broader debates about
postmodern methods and approaches to research and writing in sport
history that were aired in other forums and publications.[37]

Despite an undercurrent of criticism, if not scepticism, within the
academic community, the quickening of interest in the connections
between sport and spirituality has continued. Evidence for this can
be seen in the recent establishment of two university research centres,

---

37. For details of these ongoing debates, notably involving exchanges between Synthia
Sydnor and Allen Guttmann (and others), see comments in Sydnor's article in
this issue of *Interface*. See also Booth, *op cit*, Synthia Sydnor, 'Contact With God,
Body, and Soul: Sport History and the Radical Orthodoxy Project', in MG Phillips,
Deconstructing Sport History: A Postmodern Analysis (Albany, NY: State University of
New York Press, 2006), 203–26, and Allen Guttmann, 'Review Essay: The Ludic and
the Ludicrous', in *International Journal of the History of Sport*, 25/1 (January 2008),
100–12.

namely the Centre for Sport, Spirituality and Character Development, at Neumann College, Philadelphia, in the United States, and the Centre for the Study of Sport and Spirituality at York St John University College, York, in England.[38] The official launch of the latter centre coincided with a conference on sport and spirituality at York in August 2007. Significantly, the call for papers specified that 'perspectives from all major western and eastern faith traditions and humanistic/transcendent accounts of spirituality' were welcome (although the website later acknowledged that 'Although the Centre operates in a multi-faith context and acknowledges the value of all world religions, much of its intellectual work is currently focused on the intersection between sport and the Christian faith').[39] Over 70 delegates from eleven different countries attended the symposium, and one of the outcomes was a resolve to establish an academic peer-review journal, the *International Journal of Religion and Sport*, in order to 'promote interdisciplinary scholarship and research in the field'.[40]

A natural corollary of these conferences and research centres has been an apparent upsurge in the number of tertiary subjects and courses based on the spiritual dimensions of sport, leisure and exercise.[41] Given the

---

38. Details of the two centres are available on their respective websites. See http://www.neumann.edu/academics/special/sscd.asp and http://sportspirituality.yorksj.ac.uk.

39. See 'Call for Papers: Inaugural International Conference on Sport and Spirituality', email correspondence circulated by Nick Watson, 3 November 2006.

40. Watson and White, *op cit*, 76. In explaining the genesis of these research centres, Watson and White also cite the influence of the Christian Society for Kinesiology and Leisure Studies. Established in the United States in the late 1980s, this organisation has conducted conferences and published proceedings on the basis of its desire to 'integrate faith, sport and leisure through the sharing of scholarly work and fellowship'. Relevant publications include, *Physical Education, Sports, and Wellness: Looking to God as We Look at Ourselves*, edited by J Byl and T Visker (Sioux Center, IA: Dordt College Press, 1999), and *Christianity and Leisure: Issues in a Pluralistic Society*, edited by G Van Andel, P Heintzman and T Visker (Sioux Center, IA: Dordt College Press, 2005).

41. See Watson and White, *op cit*, 76. For information relating to undergraduate modules and postgraduate supervision in the field of sport and spirituality at the centres in York St John University College and Neumann College, see http://sportspirituality.yorksj.ac.uk and http://www.neumann.edu/academics/special/sscd.asp. There is evidence of such developments occurring in Australia. For instance, former Olympian Richard Pengelly was instrumental in establishing a subject entitled

textbook flavour of the three anthologies discussed above, it seems that a small niche 'market' in tertiary institutions had been catered for over the last decade and a half, but with the establishment of research centres, the staging of regular conferences and the launch of a new journal, a more solid foundation now exists for students to pursue formal studies in the area.

Conclusions

This brief overview of aspects of the broad relationship between sport and religion has been based on a selective survey of how academic interest in the field has manifested itself. Explicitly theological literature and debates have not been considered. By using the historiography of social science disciplines generally, and the discipline of sport history specifically, it has been possible to trace how developments in academic literature, conferences and courses have coalesced in a specific, and more recent, academic focus on matters pertaining to sport and spirituality. It is clear, however, that the current landscape in this field is still very much contested terrain. Not only do critics continue to question the academic relevance and credibility of studies in the area, but the recent emphasis by academics on what may be classified as the psycho-social aspects of sport and spirituality is still in its infancy, and may yet be supplanted by other foci. Despite these concerns, there continues to be a steady flow of literature, and a latent desire by scholars and students to pursue studies of the subject matter. It is these determinants that will hopefully continue to provide the impetus for future scholarly inquiry.

'Sport and Spirituality', now being taught at the University of Western Australia. See Brendan O'Keefe, 'UWA Resurrects Sport's Spiritual Parallels', *Australian*, 8 November 2006, 25.

Chapter Two

'When I Run I Feel God's Pleasure': Towards A Protestant Play Ethic

Gordon Preece

In the 1981 Oscar-winning film *Chariots of Fire,*[1] the film's hero Eric Liddell is literally running late for a mission meeting in a stark old Presbyterian church on a dark Edinburgh Sunday. Liddell apologises to his dour sister Jenny only to be delivered a real serve about his being perpetually distracted from the mission. Liddell then seeks to ease Jenny's worries concerning his vocation to the mission field, but after he runs in the Olympics. It is impossible to capture the passion and the Scottish accent on the page, but he says: 'God made me *fast*, Jenny, and when I run, I feel God's pleasure'. Whether Liddell actually made the statement in the film to Jenny (or her to him[2]), it has the whiff of truth in terms of his overall philosophy.

Ian Charleson, who played Liddell in the film, described Liddell's inimitable running style of 'all arms and legs and head thrown wildly back . . . in the sheer exultation of the race' as due to the fact that '"He ran with faith. He didn't even look where he was going"'.[3] Liddell's alleged statement is not only a magnificent moment in film, but in theology. It provides a stimulus for a long-overdue Protestant[4] Play Ethic which I

---

1. Directed by David Puttnam for 20ᵗʰ Century Fox.
2. Sally Magnusson, *The Flying Scotsman* (London: Quartet, 1981), 30–31: 'Contrary to the impression suggested by the film . . . there was never any opposition from the family to his athletics. "We were all thrilled to bits about his running", says his sister Jenny, who feels a little hurt at being portrayed in the film as a rather schoolmarmish character who tried to get Eric to concentrate more on his religion. "I was a naive, unsophisticated teenager at the time. I would never have dreamed of telling Eric what to do."'
3. Magnusson, *Flying Scotsman*, 14–15.
4. A standard definition of Protestantism is 'the system of Christian faith and practice based on the acceptance of the principles of the Reformation. The term is derived

will attempt to outline in this article.[5] I will firstly define play in relation to work and culture. I will then set play in the context of a theology of divine and human pleasure. I will finally narrate certain forms of play as pleasurable ends in themselves, firstly the personal, female story of Stephanie Paulsell's running and then the more corporate one of Credo Cricket, critiquing various utilitarian perversions of play as mere means to an end.

Defining play and its place in life

Defining play, like other fundamental forms of human existence like love and work, is difficult, but not impossible. Eminent child psychologist Jean Piaget notes succinctly that play is always done 'for the pleasure of the activity'.[6] It is clear that Liddell plays when he runs, for all his strenuous effort and competitive spirit.

---

from the protestation of the reforming members of the Diet of Speyer (1529) against the Catholic majority' (*Oxford Dictionary of the Christian Church*, edited by FL Cross and EA Livingstone (Oxford: Oxford University Press, 1974), 1135. A negative definition sees it as non- Roman Catholic. However, given the common scriptural heritage of Protestants and Catholics and the shared inheritance of the first five ecumenical church councils at least, this is not that helpful. While primarily presenting a counterpoint to Weber's Protestant Work Ethic, I am well aware of the variations within Protestantism. Thus I will be using Protestant to refer primarily to Reformed or Calvinistic Protestants, given Liddell's (and incidentally, my own) Presbyterian roots.

5.   For other contributions I have attempted towards such a project see my 'Re-Creation and Recreation in the 80s' in *Faith Active in Love*, edited by John Diesendorf (AFES, 1981); 'Sacred Sport', in *On Being*, (April 1983): 28–30; 'Leisurely thoughts on a Protestant Play Ethic', in *Salt*, (Summer 1986): 4–6; 'No Time for Games. Nowhere to Play,' in *Southern Cross* (February 1989): 10–11; 'Spirituality and Sport', in *Zadok Perspectives* 68, (Spring 2000): 2. Other recent works that inform my perspective are John Quilter, 'The Notion of Achievement in Sport and Some Ethical Issues in Professional Sport', in *Australian Journal of Professional and Applied Ethics*, 6/22 (September 2004): 75–88 and Pat Kane, *The Play Ethic: A Manifesto for a Different Way of Living* (London: Macmillan, 2004).

6.   *Play, Dreams and Imitation in Childhood*, translated by C Gattegno and FM Hodgson (New York: Norton, 1962), 92–93.

Johan Huizinga grasps some of the key features of play. For him play is:

> A free activity, that is standing quite consciously outside 'ordinary' life as being 'not serious', but at the same time absorbing the player intensely and utterly. 'It is an activity connected with no material interest, and no profit can be gained by it. It proceeds within its own proper boundaries of time and space according to fixed rules and in an orderly manner. It promotes the formation of social groupings.'[7]

To define play we need to also define work. This is not to say one is primary and the other secondary, merely that they are paired, are symbiotic, and 'play' off each other. Pope John Paul II defined work too widely as equivalent to all human activity that is, including play. It is 'everything that man accomplishes, whatever its nature or attendant circumstances' including procuring sustenance, developing arts and sciences, enhancing 'moral and cultural standards'.[8]

Miroslav Volf's simpler and stricter definition of work is 'an instrumental activity serving the satisfaction of [creaturely] needs', outside our own need for the activity itself. Leisure is excluded as activity done mainly for itself—perhaps as a secondary goal to meeting needs, despite subjective overlap with work along a spectrum, for example in 'a useful hobby'.[9]

In clarifying the outstanding characteristics and overlap between work and play, an analogy with eating is perhaps helpful. Eating has necessary or needy aspects for survival, social aspects and aesthetic or enjoyment aspects. 'Work, like eating, while primarily a necessity for survival and social flourishing, can and should secondarily be enjoyed in itself'. Leisure (including play), like eating, has all three aspects—we need leisure or refreshing, restful activity or inactivity, we have social leisure as relational beings and we can enjoy rest and recreation. Play

---

7. *Homo Ludens* (Boston: Beacon Press, 1955), 13.
8. *Laborem Exercens: Encyclical Letter of the Supreme Pontiff on Human Work* (London: Catholic Truth Society, 1981), 1.
9. *Work in the Spirit: Toward a Theology of Work* (New York: Oxford University Press, 1991), 11–13.

as a sub-category of leisure or rest is primarily concerned with active enjoyment, but is social and can reflect certain needs, especially when it is paid. This would be significant if we had space to look at professional play or sport—as analogous to a useful hobby.[10]

The broader notion of calling or vocation may include things done, like the best needful work and needless play, for their intrinsic value.[11] The Protestant Reformers saw vocation as a playful delight[12]—which, despite 'puritanical' distortions and stereotypes, could include vacation, leisure or play. The whole of human existence is a means 'to glorify God' as in the Westminster Shorter Catechism's first question, but this by no means diminishes our enjoyment of God or our leisure, as Liddell knew. His abstaining from running the 1924 Olympic 100 metres on Sunday expressed his glorifying God and recognition of the Sabbath's and God's grounding of all enjoyment. So, when he ran and won the 400 metres in world record time, he presumably 'felt God's pleasure', though the winning was not necessary. God delights in humans enjoying and fulfilling their created nature and gifts. The means echo the end and there is mutual divine and human pleasure.[13]

---

10. This section draws on Gordon R Preece, *The Viability of the Vocation Tradition* (Lewiston NY: Edwin Mellen, 1998), 5–6.

11. Christopher Lasch, *The True and Only Heaven: Progress and its Critics* (New York: Norton & Co, 1991), 522.

12. Volf, *Work*, 198 cf Martin Luther *Weimar Arbeit* 42:78, 4f and John Calvin, *Commentaries on the First Book of Moses called Genesis* (Grand Rapids: Eerdmans, 1948), 125.

13. God's pleasure in us is captured well in Marilynne Robinson's 2005 Pulitzer prize-winning novel *Gilead* (New York: Farrar, Strauss and Giroux, 2004), 141–2 in the aged clergyman John Ames' last testament to his son: 'Calvin says somewhere that each of us is an actor on a stage and God is the audience. That metaphor has always interested me, because it makes us artists of our own behaviour, and the reaction of God to us might be thought of as aesthetic rather than morally judgmental in the ordinary sense . . . I do like Calvin's image, though, because it suggests how God might actually enjoy us. I believe we think about that far too little. It would be a way into understanding essential things, since presumably the world exists for God's enjoyment . . . as you enjoy the *being* of a child even when in every way he is a thorn in your heart'. Cf 131where Ames remembers his youthful sporting vigour. 'Whenever I remember Edward, I think of playing catch in a hot street and that wonderful weariness of the arms. I think of leaping after a high throw and that

Karl Barth relativises work as 'significant play' in relation to the real work of reconciliation accomplished by Christ. In the light of God's coming kingdom, culture and work are serious, but not too serious.[14] Barth's love of Mozart typifies this playfulness and lack of ultimate seriousness.[15] Lest we take sport too seriously, Barth stresses the eschatological limit in the Sabbath and resurrection over against a cultural Protestant ethic that can make sport into a moralistic work. The 'true work of culture' including sport is not 'an unending process that reaches into the infinite' of God's Kingdom. Work, culture and sport have a provisional, playful sense (anticipating Barth's Ethics of Redemption in relation to art and humour), lest we view them too solemnly as a collegial cooperation with God.[16]

We can compare liturgy, and especially the eucharist, as playful 'like the serious play of children' as Elizabeth Newman says. She cites Swiss reformed theologian Jean-Jacques von Allmen who depicts liturgy as 'an eschatological game'. This is not something trivial to be taken lightly. No, it's serious, but serious and joyful play. Worship like a game has rules. People are expected to give their best. 'And like other games, worship has its own purpose, which is humankind's chief end, "to glorify God and enjoy Him forever"'.[17] Liturgical, public worship is meant to flow over into and flavour our daily, informal worship (Rom 12:1, 2), at work and play.

In the chapter 'The Metaphysics of Sports' in his book *The Joy of Sports*, Catholic thinker Michael Novak says forthrightly: 'Play, not work, is the

---

wonderful collaboration of the whole body with itself and that wonderful certainty and amazement that you know the glove is just where it should be. Oh, I will miss the world!' Cf Suzanne Schreiner, *The Theatre of His Glory: Nature and the Natural Order in the Thought of John Calvin* (Grand Rapids: Baker, 1995).

14.   Karl Barth, 'The Christian's Place in Society', in his *The Word of God and the Word of Man*, translated Douglas Horton (Boston and Chicago: Pilgrim Press, 1928), 311–12, 323.

15.   See Karl Barth, *Wolfgang Amadeus Mozart*, translated by CK Pott, foreword J Updike (Grand Rapids: Eerdmans, 1986), 16, 22. Cf Preece, *Viability*, 153, fn13.

16.   Karl Barth, *Ethics* (New York: Seabury, 1981), 216–23, especially 222–3, cf 490, 504–5.

17.   Elizabeth Newman, *Untamed Hospitality: Welcoming God and Other Strangers* (Grand Rapids: Brazos, 2007), 159.

end of life. To participate in the rites of play is to dwell in the Kingdom of Means . . . In a Protestant culture, as in Marxist cultures, work is serious, important, adult. Its essential insignificance is overlooked . . . play is reality. Work is diversion and escape'.[18] Novak is not nuanced. As a Catholic he enjoys putting down the Protestant Work Ethic. But his point that play is an end, with a purpose in itself, is well taken.

Novak states categorically that sports are not just part of life, they are the heart of life. '[T]he heart of human reality is courage, honesty, freedom, community, excellence: the heart is sports'. Yet it is not the only end, Novak notes. 'Sports are not, of course, all of life'—but they are its ethical essence. The virtues generated from sports should 'inform one's family life, civic life, political life, work life... What the person of wisdom needs to derive from every sphere of life is its inherent beauty, attraction, power, force . . .' Sports civilize. 'Sports are the highest products of civilization and the most accessible, lived, experiential sources of the civilizing spirit . . . Cease play, cease civilization'.[19]

Novak's defence of sport as an end in itself and his affirmation of the sporting virtues is well taken. However, his inter-religious critique, broad civilisational generalizations, and absolutisation of American sports (in the way the baseball World Series can be used to describe a purely US competition), risks going to the opposite extreme, his minor caveat aside. Sports may not be all of life, but they clearly make a totalising, imperial claim in his view. This endangers the nature of other spheres of life as ends in themselves. Barth, Newman and von Allmen are better

---

18. Michael Novak, *The Joy of Sports* (Lanham MD: Hamilton Press, 1967), 40.
19. Novak, *The Joy of Sports*, 40–43. Even more starkly Novak says on page xii: 'The basic reality of all human life is play, games, sport; these are the realities from which the basic metaphors for all that is important in the rest of life are drawn . . . Art, prayer, worship, love, civilization: these thrive in the field of play . . . 'Barbarians play in order to work; the civilized work in order to play'. The severe Puritan bias of America leads us to under-value sports. America took root in Protestant culture, and as de Tocqueville noted in 1836, Americans did not play, had no sports, centered their lives in work. As America has grown more Catholic, more Jewish, more various, the world of play has acquired intellectual traditions here. The nation needs a post-Protestant understanding of itself. At the heart of its rejuvenation may lie sports'.

Important as character-building and Christian witness are as by-products of sporting involvement, it concerns goods external to the internal goods of sport itself—the very 'spirituality' of sport—'when Melissa King briefly enjoys the grace of athletic excellence and the joy of community with complete strangers'. In the 2005 book *She's Got Next: Life Under the Net*, King spells out why she loves pick-up basketball in ways that have much in common with Liddell, despite the absence of explicit reference to God. Nonetheless, it's a pre-echo of eternity or a 'signal of transcendence' to use Peter Berger's terms.[32]

> I've played because, when the game is good, when everyone is doing, not thinking, it happens, little stillnesses in the moments when you see your open man and nothing else, or you feel your shot going in the hoop as it leaves your hands, or you share a laugh with someone you've never spoken to. Race, money, gender, age, they're still there. But the junk we're all saddled with is gone.[33]

From a more explicit Christian perspective the grace or aesthetic excellence of shared bodily exercise can help eradicate a passive sense of entertainment that distracts us from coming to terms with the 'junk' of our alienated, mortal bodies and the baptismal practice that enables us to come to terms with them. A 'baptismal imagining of the body'[34] and the practice of giving our bodies over to a dying and rising with Christ for God's and our pleasure, provides a link between spirituality and sport, from the more basic forms like walking to the more sophisticated forms like professional athletics.

---

the second Sydney: Strand, 1999.

32. *Rumor of Angels: Modern Society and the Rediscovery of the Supernatural* (Garden City NY: Doubleday Anchor, 1970), 52–53.

33. I owe much of this section and the King quote to Mark Galli, 'The Grace of Sports', http:www.christianitytoday.com/ct/2005/109/52.0.html posted 03/05/2005.

34. Ian Barns, 'Living Christianly in a Technological World', in *Zadok Papers* S 152 (Autumn 2007): 6.

As Christine Ledger notes (before citing Albert Borgmann in full):

> Physical activities, from the simple to the athletic, from a
> brisk walk to a marathon, remind us of both the abilities
> and the limitations of the body. Physical activities, practiced
> alone or with others, require discipline and repeated effort
> in a technological society where ease of transport and
> passive entertainment are encouraged. However, they
> engage us with our bodies and with the world in a way
> cars and television do not.[35]

Borgmann elaborates the example of running this way:

> Running is simply to move through time and space, step-
> by-step. But there is a splendor in that simplicity. In a car we
> move of course much faster, farther and more comfortably.
> But we are not moving on our own power and in our own
> right. We cash in prior labor for present motion. Being
> beneficiaries of science and engineering and having worked
> to pay for a car, gasoline, and roads, we now release what
> has been stored and use it for transportation. What I am
> doing now, driving, requires no effort, and little or no skill
> or discipline. I am a divided person; my achievement lies
> in the past, my enjoyment in the present. But in the runner,
> effort and joy are one; the split between means and ends,
> labor and leisure is healed . . . the runner is mindful of the
> body because the body is intimate with the world. The mind
> becomes relatively disembodied when the body is severed
> from the depth of the world when the world is split into
> commodious surfaces and inaccessible machineries. Thus
> the unity of ends and means, of mind and body, and of
> body and the world is one and the same. It makes itself

---

35.   Christine Ledger, 'Creativity, Community and Technology', in *God Down Under:*
      Theology in the Antipodes, edited by Winifred Wing Han Lamb and Ian Barns
      (Adelaide: ATF Press, 2003), 163.

felt in the vividness with which the runner experiences reality.[36]

While Liddell is more succinct and simple, he would have wholeheartedly agreed. Our challenge today is not to produce more Olympians, but more ordinary runners and walkers who can 'feel God's pleasure' for themselves and not merely by the proxy of passive entertainment of technology and 'disabling professions' as Ivan Illich puts it.[37]

Today's professional problematising of ordinary bodies under the rubric of what Joan Jacobs Brumberg calls 'the body project'[38] is a far cry from Liddell's relatively lazy amateurism, for the love of it. Our grim sporting obsession with the work ethic takes the body as a technologically modifiable task, not a gift. The perversion of this is seen in the recent tragedy of Marion Jones' glorious smile at the Sydney Olympics turning to tears this year as she admitted to taking performance enhancing drugs.[39] Another exhilarating athlete Florence Griffith-Joyner, nicknamed Flo Jo, remained under a similar cloud before and after her untimely death.

While not a case of using drugs, the thrilling record-equalling sixteenth straight test victory by the Australian cricket team, against a luckless India, victim of bad umpiring and a refusal of key Australian batsmen, captain Ricky Ponting and the match-winning Andrew Symonds, to walk when they knew they were clearly out, left a bad taste in the mouth and bad spirit between the teams and questions about the lost spirit(uality?) of the game. As Michael Costello wrote:

> The responsibility for this win-at-all-costs approach doesn't lie so much with Symonds, a wonderful cricketer, as with those who have been responsible in recent decades

---

36.   Ledger, 'Creativity, Community and Technology', 164-5 citing Albert Borgmann, *Technology and the Character of Contemporary Life: A Philosophical Inquiry* (Chicago: The University of Chicago Press, 1984), 202-3.

37.   Ivan Illich, 'Disabling Professions', in his *The Right to Useful Unemployment and its Professional Enemies* (London: Marion Boyars, 1978).

38.   Cited in Stephanie Paulsell, *Honoring the Body: Meditations on a Christian Practice* (San Francisco: Jossey-Bass, 2002), 125.

39.   '"Punished" Jones pleads for Leniency', in *The Australian*, January 4, 2008, Sport, 24.

for the game becoming more and more driven above all by the dollar. The whatever-it-takes approach may lead to more victories on the scorecard, but in the end, it leads to a troubled spirit.[40]

The players defended themselves self-righteously and were defended by many, legalistically and fatalistically, in terms of the rules, the umpire's call being final, luck evening itself out etc. Others called for technological fixes, another attempt to avoid human responsibility for upholding the spirit, character and end of the game, that was taken for granted until recent times, and has recently been upheld by walkers West Indian Brian Lara and Australian Adam Gilchrist.[41]

One humane antidote to this terrible obsession with full-time technological professionalism or 'the body project' is the weekly Jewish strike known as the sabbath. It regularly reminds us that our bodies and lives are gifts. It is ironic that in *Chariots of Fire*, the in many ways admirable Jewish athlete Harold Abrahams, who had to overcome anti-Semitism, and won the 100 metres at the 1924 Olympics with Liddell sidelined, is painted as such a product of the Protestant Work Ethic. He tells his coach he'd always been afraid of losing before, but now he was afraid of winning—'ten lonely seconds to justify my whole existence'.

---

40. 'To Walk or not to Walk, That is the Question', in *The Australian*, (January 4, 2008), 10.

41. *Ibid*, 10. Cf Indian captain Anil Kumble's comment 'only one team is playing in the spirit of the game', ('Kumble's Bodyline Bouncer' *The Australian*, Jan 7, 2008, 15) echoing the immortal words of Australia's Bodyline series captain Bill Woodfull when England's fast bowlers continually bowled at the bodies of Australian batsmen. A loss of the spirit of the game is not only cricket's problem. Similarly, Jesus' question of 'what does it profit a person if they gain the whole world but lose their soul?' is put well in a football (soccer) and corporate context by Brian Draper to Tom Hicks, the brash billionaire and new highly leveraged owner of the iconic Liverpool Football Club, now corporation. Just before Liverpool's loss to AC Milan in the 2007 Champions League Final he said: 'When . . . we bought Weetabix . . . we leveraged it up to make our return. You could say anyone who was eating Weetabix was paying for our purchase of Weetabix. It was just business. It is the same for Liverpool. Revenues come in from whatever source and go out to whatever source, and if there's money left over, it is profit'. Draper gets the last word: 'What price football if we reduce its story to the dimensions of a Weetabix?' www.licc.org.uk/culture/the-business-of-football posted May 25 2007.

Meanwhile Liddell was so committed to the Christian (and Scottish!) Sabbath that he refused to run in his favourite 100 metre sprint event because it was scheduled on a Sunday, but won the 400 metres gold on another day. Sabbath-keeping, which is so often painted legalistically, is in fact for Liddell and the Jews, the tap-root for a proper theology of play, imitating God's own playful sabbath satisfaction with creation.

Stephanie Paulsell's story of recovering pleasure in running

To uphold Liddell's spirit of bodily enjoyment and counteract the corroding effects of the professional and technological 'body project' we need both individual and corporate models or 'performances' of the kind of narrative we are advocating. Harvard Divinity School ministry lecturer Stephanie Paulsell captures brilliantly the sense of unselfconscious child-like enjoyment of bodily exercise and the ways that adolescent, especially female self-conciousness and adult productivity diminish it. Her story and insights are worth quoting at length.

> I remember childhood joy in bodily exertion—especially in swimming and dancing. I remember also the dilution of that joy and its gradual replacement with self-consciousness about my body and reluctance to exert myself – at least in the presence of others.
>
> . . . I was a slow runner, always coming in last. So, naturally, I was assigned to a footrace during our seventh-grade field day. I confided my fears about this race to my mother who loved to run. She began running before the running craze began . . . in white thin-soled Keds (this was also before the running-shoe craze began). 'Wear my sneakers!' she said. 'They are soft and light, and you'll feel like you're running on air'.
>
> So I did. I wore her white Keds with the soft thin soles. And she was right: I felt as light as a whisper, fast and strong. I flew toward the finish line thinking, 'So *this* is what it feels like to run *fast!*' But when I crossed it I was greeted with wild laughter and and shouts of 'Windmill!' Evidently what I had experienced as speed and strength had looked, instead, like a girl careening down her lane

with her arms flailing. The name 'Windmill' followed me
for years, and I began to take care never to be seen running.
I began to slow down.[42]

It is interesting to compare Paulsell's 'windmill' with the earlier
description of Liddell as 'all arms and legs and head thrown wildly back
. . . in the sheer exultation of the race'. Perhaps it was acceptable for a
man, not a woman. Maybe winning made the difference. Or perhaps
it was a time when we were less conscious of proper running style.
Whatever it was, what a shame that Paulsell lost the joy of running –
though not for good.

It was a long time before I again felt the joy I felt running
in my mother's shoes. But in graduate school I fell in
love with a man who ran with effortless grace, who took
pleasure both in the steady rhythms of a long run and the
lung-expanding, leg-pounding exhilaration of a sprint . . . .
Finally, one night he said . . . 'let's go to the gym and run,
it'll feel so good' . . . [43]

His suggested slow start, a mile and a half run was something she'd
never done. He coached and challenged, through the pain barrier till
finally finishing with a sprint.
Paulsell picks up at this point:

And in a burst of energy, I did. I sprinted down the last
half of the track, Kevin matching me stride for stride, and
felt in every muscle the pleasure of exertion, of pushing
my body beyond its boundaries. It was a physical pleasure,
the pleasure of feeling myself wholly embodied, of feeling
blood and breath moving through me. It was a spiritual
pleasure, the relief of feeling old fears and inhibitions
drained of their power, a feeling of freedom and possibility.
And it was a sexual pleasure, the pleasure of feeling
someone I love drawing out my strength, urging me on,

---

42.   Paulsell, *Honoring the Body*, 114–15.
43.   *Ibid*, 115.

matching his body's rhythms to mine. It is one of my husband's enduring gifts to me that he reintroduced me to the joy of bodily exertion. Through honoring my body and its strength, he helped me begin to do the same.[44]

Reflecting on Scripture's rapturous perspective on the human body 'made in God's image' (Gen 1:27), 'fearfully and wonderfully made' (Ps 139:14), and 'a temple of the Holy Spirit' (1 Cor 6:9), Paulsell notes from painful personal experience that 'it is the rare person who is moved to praise by the scrutiny of his or her own body'. The bodies of others, however, do sometimes evoke our praise and wonderment. And often they do this through feats of bodily exertion. 'Think of Michael Jordan flying toward the basket, ball controlled by one outstretched hand, all his muscles taut. Think of Olympic runners and swimmers, gymnasts and skaters, beautiful in their strength and speed'.

Yet she affirms the pleasure of sheer participation against all temptation to armchair perfectionism.

I certainly can't play basketball like Michael Jordan, but I can test my limits in a basketball game with friends . . . I'll never be as graceful as Isadora Duncan, but when my daughter and I put on music and dance our hearts out, we do taste joy. Everyone's limits are different—some press against them from the seats of their wheelchairs, some on the slopes of high mountains, some in the streets and parks of their neighborhood. The history of the body is the history of its own striving to surpass itself . . .

You don't have to be a world-class athlete to experience the pleasure of embodiment through vigorous exertion. You have only to embrace some activity that allows you to feel your heart beating, your blood pulsing, your breath drawn in and released . . . [45]

---

44.   *Ibid*, 116.
45.   *Ibid*, 117.

But as Borgmann reminded us, it takes the disciplined effort of practice or MacIntyre's social practices to burst out of our technological envelope. For Paulsell, 'unless our livelihood depends upon manual labor, we must *choose*, deliberately to exert ourselves. "Here come the joggers", writes Galway Kinnell in his poem 'The Tragedy of Bricks'.

> They run for fun through a world where everyone used to
> lay bricks
> For work.
> Their faces tell there is a hell and they will reach it.[46]

In our sedentary, obesity-inducing cities, like Kinnell's joggers we have to make extraordinary efforts to exercise our bodies when once it was a part of ordinary life. Compare the way art has been professionalized above the level of ordinary objects of craft, like Shaker chairs.

Again as Paulsell reminds us, if we want to glorify and enjoy our bodies and enable those of our children likewise, we must sustain 'the natural delight' we take in youthful movement across our lifespan: 'we honor our bodies as God's creation when we inhabit them with greater attention, for when we are where our body is, we are also where our creator is . . . When we reach and stretch and move, we have an opportunity to know ourselves fashioned by one who cherishes bodies.'[47] Liddell sustained that childlike delight. He was a man at home with his creaturely body, head kicked back, enjoying running and his Creator simultaneously.

Paulsell is learning to enjoy running like Liddell, within limitations. In a time-constrained technological and utilitarian society she describes her own practice of combining her beloved walking with speed-walking for time's sake and a quick run for aerobic fitness' sake. It's a compromise but a creative one:

> I get the aerobic exercise my body needs and the more leisurely sense of my body out and about in creation that my spirit craves. Choosing those exertions that will give us joy doesn't mean we shouldn't challenge ourselves or press

46.   *Ibid*, 122–23.
47.   *Ibid*, 124.

against our limits. Indeed, we should. But our exertions shouldn't be all hell-bound grimacing like those of Galway Kinnell's joggers. We should expect to find some pleasure waiting for us when we rouse our bodies to exercise.[48]

Paulsell provides a poignant personal and distinctively feminine perspective on bodily pleasure in running and other sports. She reflects a journey that many women undergo from childlike, God-given pleasure in physical play to adolescent alienation. She is more blessed than most to have substantially recovered that original child-like pleasure (through her husband) and to be now passing it on and enjoying it with her own child. Liddell would be pleased.[49]

Credo cricket: 'cricket you can believe in'

We turn now to a more corporate and male narrative of the recovery of pleasure in sport, obscured for long periods by experiences of disempowerment through unemployment, ultra-competitiveness, addiction, homelessness, mental illness. It is the story of Credo Cricket, an arm of Credo Café's ministry with the homeless and marginalised, a ministry of Urban Seed in the heart of Melbourne, located in Baptist Place, one of Melbourne's main heroin injecting areas, behind Collins St. Baptist Church. It is best known through the highly public profile of a previous director Tim Costello. As far as possible I will let Marcus Curnow, Credo's resident cricket tragic and coordinator, speak for the team.

Credo cricket began in 2001 in Melbourne parks and laneways as a way of building relationships and beating some of the pressures of depression and addiction. As Curnow's inimitable My Space TV account (the best way to follow it) puts it:

---

48.   *Ibid*, 129.
49.   For less profound but secular, practical, earthy wisdom that largely confirms and complements the perspective represented here, see Amby Burfoot, *The Runner's Guide to the Meaning of Life* (Rodale Inc, 2000) and Simon Barnes, *The Meaning of Sport* (London: Short Books, 2006). Also note Wayne Booth, *For the Love of It: Amateuring and its Rivals* (Chicago: University of Chicago Press, 2000); Haruki Murakami, *What I talk About When I Talk About Running* (London: Harvill Secker, 2008).

It's about Jonno who's pushing for state selection playing on the same team as Gilly pushing for refugee status. It's about getting a different kind of hit in the lane. It's getting enough money from church on Christmas Day because you're homeless and then spending it on a ticket to the Boxing Day [Cricket] Test . . . it's also about finding out the scorer is illiterate and no-one knows who won, but it doesn't matter . . . It's about the face of the opposition captain when the bloke in the wheelchair asks if he can bat with a runner. It's the lessons you've never had an opportunity to learn, finding out the accountant in the corporate team was once homeless himself. It's Credo Cricket. It's very believable.

In Credo cricket the last very often ends up being first as in the recent last game of the regular indoor season, facing the top team. We hadn't won a game, the guys were dispirited. Marcus, the captain and coach was out injured, as was another regular, Dave. A group of visiting Samoan-Kiwi youth workers (who have their own indigenised, hybrid game of cricket) provided raucous support with Samoan chants. And we won in the last over. There were rapturous scenes. Winning isn't everything, but it is something, and it's nice to have the occasional one to savour. (Even Liddell had a fierce sense of competition). If I heard the story once I heard it twenty times. Like the Australian skater who won Winter Olympics gold after all the other competitors fell over, we made the semis (due to dropouts) and lost, but that last game of the season will be long remembered.

If that is the narrative form of Credo Cricket, of a kind of almost eschatological, last- shall-be-first enjoyment, below is the credal form entitled *'Our Cricket Credo'*:

Fair go: 'Everybody get's their $10 worth'. Equality of opportunity and enabling participation is more important than sporting brilliance.

Giving one's personal best on and off the field.

We seek to give every opportunity for individuals to achieve their personal best.

Life is a team game. We need each other!

Give opportunity for people to improve in order to get better at cricket, the arts of the game and life.

Team success and achievement of an individual is always relative to community (that is, some champions and 'Premiers' are losers).

The 'spirit' with which we play the game IS the result.

The team with the best stories at the end of the day is the real winner.

There is always hope because cricket (like life) is a funny game.

Credo are the 'Fun Premiers' every year.

It's easier to be the fun premiers if you are the actual premiers . . . that is, being competitive is more fun that getting slaughtered.

Lunch/Tea/Drinks breaks are as important as the game.

Everyone should get a chance to bowl 'The Gatting Ball'.[50]

Cricket is a great leveller!

Failure is an important part of success.

Sledging happens . . . it could be art or abuse.

Sledge unto others only as you would have them sledge unto you.

We seek to love our enemies! Your opponent is often your shadow side.

(OK, These last two we adapted from Jesus, who obviously selected 12 blokes as a good number for a team with cricket in mind) . . .

Formation of meaningful and significant relationships.

Priority for those normally excluded from cricket cultures and society.

---

50.   The famous Shane Warne delivery on his English Test debut that bowled bemused England captain Mike Gatting around his legs.

Honesty in evaluation of our abilities, strengths and weaknesses.

Variety is the spice of cricket: If a quick is getting carted put on a spinner; if a thin guy is getting carted, put on a fat guy; if a bloke is getting carted put on a woman; if someone good is getting carted put on someone ordinary . . . etc etc.

Nothing too strenuous: 'If you play cricket well there should be no need to run!'

Sometimes it's cricket you can believe in and at other times it's just very believable cricket!'[51]

Credo Cricket recently received funding to take this credo, this spirit of 'backyard' cricket into the laneways of Melbourne 'to expand and enhance the possibilities of assisting marginalised people to become involved with physical activity as well as reaping the benefits of belonging to a team'. Some of these benefits cited in the application included:

- A person who has been long-term unemployed feels encouraged by the skills gained through the cricket team and supported by staff and volunteers on the team to seek and obtain part-time employment as a secondary school cricket coach.
- A person who has experienced restrictions in life due to unhealthy habits and long term mental health issues is invited to play . . . cricket. Whilst deciding that Credo Cricket is too demanding, the person is motivated by involvement in the team to lose weight, give up smoking and take up a more active lifestyle.
- A homeless person who attends a Credo Cricket game because they have nowhere to stay is supported by other team members to obtain crisis accommodation . . . This occurs on another three occasions over the course of the season before stable housing is found.
- An asylum seeker with limited English language skills gains confidence in experience of Australian culture.
- Homeless people and business people participate in a corporate cricket match. Through the experience of playing cricket,

---

51.   See www.myspace.com/credocricket

sharing lunch and hearing the Credo Cricket story told, negative stereotypes of each other are broken down.

- Through partnership with a local cricket club, Urban Seed raises awareness about the barriers to participation faced by marginalised people, and mediates in the process of the club becoming more inclusive.
- Marginalised people build relationships beyond welfare circles.[52]
- 'Sporting activity and belonging to a team are a vital source of social capital'.[53]

Research on health inequality, social exclusion and social epidemiology connects physical activity and team spirit with long term health and social gains. These ideas have been highlighted recently by The Big Issue's Street Socceroos and Reclink's Choir of Hard Knocks'. Credo Cricket is the Cricket of Hard Knocks.

Despite the somewhat more bureaucratic, utilitarian language of a funding application grant, and after much debate about how not to lose Credo Cricket's distinctive ethos of play and community as ends in themselves, it has managed to maintain much of that ethos, even in the application. As mentioned earlier, Credo Cricket started as a form of backyard or street cricket—a venerable tradition in Australia. It has been maintained over five years by people (particularly Marcus Curnow) who are passionate for the game. Credo Cricket has had minimal funding. It is amateurism in its purest form—for the love (and occasional hate) of the game. Statistics are less significant than stories. Stories are much more about means and the character of the game, team and player corresponding to ends. Statistics are all about ends justifying means, where consequentialism conquers. Nothing could be less 'useful' or utilitarian than 'mad dogs and Englishmen', and the occasional refugee, 'out in the midday sun'.

---

52.   Written by Kate Allen and Marcus Curnow, September, 2007.
53.   See 'Dropping off the Edge', Jesuit Social Services in Australia, 2007.

Conclusion

This paper has used the filmic Eric Liddell's quotation 'When I run, I feel God's pleasure', as a stepping-stone to a sporting theology of pleasure as 'enjoying God'. Apart from some technical definitions, it has largely used a narrative theology approach to flesh out or embody such a theology. The stories of Stephanie Paulsell and Credo Cricket largely speak for themselves as exemplars of a Liddell-like spirituality of sport, of bodily enjoyment of God and creation as an alternative to the constraints of modern, professionalised, technologised sport.

Let me conclude with one last story. One of the highlights of Credo cricket practice is playing with Adam, the adolescent son of one of our regulars, Peter. Adam cannot speak, but he's not dumb. When he bowls and bats and catches, he has the most eloquent smile and chuckle. Like Liddell and the last Adam, he feels God's pleasure.

Chapter Three

We Are The Champions! Origins And Developments Of The Image Of God's Athletes

Victor C Pfitzner

Gods and games

Modern day sportspeople and spectators might readily use the divine name or Jesus Christ as expletives of frustration or exclamations of triumph, but they would rarely make a connection between games and religion. Support for one's team might occasionally reach the heights of religious zeal but associating athletic prowess with piety would be far from the thinking of most performers and onlookers. Yet there are moments when even our modern sports spectaculars are conducted with quasi-religious rituals—think of the opening rites at the Olympic Games[1] or the singing of the obligatory 'Abide with me' at every FA Cup final in England.

That games and gods belonged together was taken for granted in the ancient world, whether at the classical Greek athletic contests of Olympia, Nemea, Pythia or Isthmia, at the dramatic contests in Athens, or at the more bellicose and brutal gladiatorial games of the Romans. Contests between the gods belong to the oldest myths of Greek literature, so it is not surprising that the origins and ideals of the great national contests were found in the myths of gods and heroes.[2] All local games (Greek, *agones*) stood under the patronage and protection of a deity; and a breach of the peace during the conduct of the games was a serious

---

1. The solemn rites conducted with white-robed 'priestesses' at ancient Olympia prior to the last Athens Olympics bore many of the marks of religious ritual.
2. See, for example, Pindar Olympian Odes X and Homer's account of the funeral games in honour of Patroclus in the Iliad, Book 23. For documentation, in ancient Greek literature, of the religious nature of the ancient games, see Victor C Pfitzner, *Paul and the Agon Motif: Traditional Athletic Imagery in the Pauline Literature*, Supplements to Novum Testamentum XVI (Leiden: E J Brill, 1967), 18–20.

offence against the deity. Contestants vowed to comply with the rules
of the games and prayed for victory before an image of the patron deity
and there the victors later laid their prizes and wreathes, the latter often
cut from a tree in the deity's adjacent sacred grove. Little wonder, then,
that the games were considered holy, as rites in which the gods were
honoured by physical and artistic achievement. All who participated,
not only the winners, were athletes of the gods. Little wonder, also, that
all public contests—not only gladiatorial—were condemned by early
Christian writers.[3]

Besides honouring the gods, the Greek games gave expression to and
fostered human values intrinsic to the Greek spirit of rivalry and self-
assertion, the desire for victory and fame. Winners were celebrated in
athletics, dramatics and in every field of endeavour. An adult male's
entire civic life gave opportunity to contest against others and to excel.
Athletic contests gave a splendid stage on which to demonstrate physical
prowess and to achieve lasting honour.[4] Such ideals were inculcated in
the Greek gymnasia whose curricula, whether literary, artistic, musical
or athletic, fostered the spirit of competition and the quest for fame.

The philosopher as *true* athlete of god

The exaggerated importance of sports in the gymnasium and the desire
for fame in the pan-Hellenic games led to a professionalism (nothing is
new!) that tended to debase the ancient noble ideals of athletics. While
the gymnasium remained an essential tool for inculcating Hellenistic
culture, the athlete increasingly became an object of scorn for tragedians,
poets and philosophers. Voices of dissent were heard early. Already in the
fifth century BCE, tragedians poured vitriol on athletes who disciplined
only their bodies,[5] while philosophers from Xenophanes to Plato and
Aristotle laid claim to strength and skill that put all the glorious victories

---

3.   See especially Tertullian *De Spectaculis* 11; *De Corona Militis* 13.
4.   Though typically Greek, such ideals lasted well into Roman times. Lucian, writing
      in the second century CE, makes Solon say to the Persian Anacharsis, with reference
      to the athlete's quest for glory: 'If anyone were to take away from life the love of
      fame, what good would still be left to us?' (*Anacharsis* 36).
5.   See Euripides *Fragments* 282N and Sophocles *Ajax* 1250. Their comments anticipate
      modern jibes against 'dumb jocks' on the part of those considering themselves to
      be intellectually superior!

of athletes in the shade. Exercise of the mind and soul was far more profitable for the individual and the polis than the exercise of the body! Every sage in search of wisdom and virtue was to be considered a better athlete than the dirty, grunting, sweating competitor vying for nothing more than ephemeral fame and a crown of laurel, myrtle or some such that would soon wilt.[6]

Plato reacted strongly against the exaggerated spirit of competition, employing the full range of athletic terminology and imagery to describe higher and nobler pursuits. The prime purpose of athletic exercise was to be preparation for war,[7] but it had its own educational value and moral worth in the development of the intellect and the formation of character. The true contest of life involved the exercise of the rational and temperamental parts of the soul in order to control one's inner desires.[8] Similarly, Aristotle frequently used the image of the runner, boxer or wrestler in his Nichomachean Ethics to illustrate the discipline and resolve required in the pursuit of the ethical mean that will result in happiness.[9]

But it was the Cynics, followed by the Stoics, who fully appropriated the athletic image to themselves. The old ideal of noble excellence (Greek, *kalok'agathia*) as exemplified in athletic achievement is now explicated in purely ethical terms. A consistent polemic against the games and athletics in general is a recurring theme of the moral discourses of late Stoics such as Epictetus, Seneca, Marcus Aurelius and Plutarch. Their repeated argument is that the only truly good, noble and heroic contest is the one waged by the wise person against fate and fortune in the pursuit of self-control and equanimity. That this moral contest is holy, and the successful sage a champion of god, follows from the fact that victory is gained by following the inner voice of divine reason. Mocking mere physical achievement as folly, the popular moral philosophers claim that they are the true champions as they struggle for virtue.[10] They contest

---

6.   For a fuller treatment of this philosophical tradition, see Pfitzner, *Paul and the Agon Motif*, 23–35.
7.   *Republic* III 403ff, 413 D.
8.   See *Phaedrus* 247 B; *Republic* X 608; *Laws* 647 C&D.
9.   *Ethics* III 12, 1117b, 2.
10. Like its Greek equivalent *arete*, the Latin *virtus* originally has connotations of masculine strength. The consistent polemic against the folly of the games and of

not against other human beings but against the vagaries of fate and their own passions. Their prize is no fading wreath but the happiness and contentment that only the pursuit of virtue brings. This is true fame and glory.

> What blows do athletes receive in their face! ... Yet they bear all the torture from thirst of glory. Let us also overcome all things, for our reward is not a crown or a palm branch or the trumpeter proclaiming silence for the announcement of our name, but virtue and strength of mind and peace acquired ever after.[11]

As they wrestle against the dominance of external circumstances, pleasure and pain they have Hercules as their patron and heroic model, taking his *labours* as allegories of the moral struggles to which all are called. Epictetus expresses a common theme: all who are intent on entering these contests are enrolled in the *true* Olympics.[12]

Jewish champions of piety

Ancient Hebrew contained no terms for athletic games; public nakedness and Greek agonistic ideals were foreign to ancient Israel. But Jewish communities living in the Hellenistic world were familiar with athletics and some, like Philo of Alexandria, would have been very familiar with athletic imagery in the service of philosophical traditions. The persistence of traditional athletic imagery is illustrated by two passages in the Wisdom of Solomon. Speaking of the pursuit of virtue, Wisdom says:

> Present, we imitate it; absent we long for it;
> Crowned, it holds triumph through eternity

---

athletes is best seen in the sayings of Diogenes as reported by Dio Chrysostom and Diogenes Laertius.

11.   Seneca *Epistles* 78.16. See Pfitzner, *Paul and the Agon Motif*, 28–37 for further references.

12.   See for example Epictetus *Dissertations* I 24,1f; III 22, 51; III 25,2f.

having striven for blameless prizes
and emerged victorious from the contest.
(4:1; Jerusalem Bible)

'Blameless prizes' continues the traditional contrast between the sage's contest for virtue and the vanity of an athlete's physical efforts. Another passage, picturing wisdom guiding Job (10:1–11:1), ends: "In an arduous struggle she awarded him the prize, to teach him that piety is stronger than all' (10:12b; JB). The reference is to Jacob's wrestling match at the brook Jabbok (Genesis 32:24–30). Sophia's role was to serve as referee and prize-giver. Interestingly, Jacob also appears in the writings of Philo of Alexandria as the athlete of God *par excellence*. In Philo, also, the contest is the struggle to maintain not just virtue, but true piety and godliness in obedience to divine direction. Interesting in this Jewish adaptation of the athletic metaphor is the concentration on the protagonist with little attention given to any antagonist.

Traditional features of Cynic-Stoic athletic imagery abound in Philo: the contrasts between the supposedly holy nature of the national games and the truly holy nature of striving for piety, between athletes who care only for sporting achievement and those who pursue higher goals.[13] God's athletes of piety are Olympic participants in the noblest contest, striving for the truly valuable crown that no festal gathering can offer. The whole range of athletic terminology and imagery become part of Philo's stock in trade to picture the self-control, discipline, renunciation, practice and effort required to achieve godliness. As in the moral diatribes of the Cynic and Stoic philosophers, comparisons with the wrestler, boxer and pancratiast dominate, but now the role of Hercules as model is replaced, in the process of allegorising Old Testament texts, by the patriarchs and other figures. Jacob is viewed as *the* type of God's athlete, but Abraham and Isaac are, with him,

---

13.   For example *On Husbandry* 113 and 119; *On the Change of Names* 106; for a fuller treatment of Philo's use of athletic imagery see Pfitzner, *Paul and the Agon Motif, 38–48.* Harold A Harris probably overstates Philo's first-hand knowledge of athletic contests in *Greek Athletics and the Jews* (Lampeter: University of Wales Press, 1976), 57. Though Herod the Great built sporting complexes at Jerusalem and Caesarea, and even endowed the Olympic games in perpetuity (*ibid*, 35, 36), such things would have been regarded as foreign by the average Judaean.

> athletes who equip themselves for the truly holy contests,
> who value lightly physical contests and take thought for
> the good condition of the soul through earnest striving for
> victory over the opposing passions. (*Migration of Abraham*
> 200)

Moses, Joseph, Enoch, Noah, even the children of Israel in their desert wanderings, become God's champions in the struggle against the dominance of human desires and passions.

Much of this sounds like a rehash of diatribal thought and diction, but Philo wants to remain a faithful Jew. Thus the struggles of God's saints in the Old Testament, and the battles of Israel against its enemies,[14] depict God's athletes as protagonists for godliness and holiness, the antagonists being anything that can destroy true piety. It is Israel's God who has set up the contest, who is the referee and awarder of prizes. God's athletes are never as self-sufficient as the Cynic-Stoic sage who prays to the divine light of reason within. They are dependent on God who remains essentially transcendent, in contrast to the Stoics' immanent 'world soul' or ruling reason that pervades all of nature. While often reverting to the familiar theme of reason versus the passions, Philo is at pains to show that the universal law of reason is perfectly embodied in the Mosaic Law.

The contest of piety is fought to the honour of God since the goal of all ethical endeavour is 'to live to God alone'.[15] For Philo, the pursuit of godliness brings its own rewards but, in contrast to the Cynic-Stoic diatribe where the image of the victor's prize or crown appears relatively rarely, Philo often refers to the prizes to be awarded God's champions of piety. One passage, using three different terms for athletic prizes, will suffice as an example:

> He [Abraham] reaches perfection with virtue as his
> instructor and receives as a prize (*athlon*) trust in God.
> To him [Isaac], who through his natural disposition and
> through independent hearing and learning has gained
> virtue, falls the prize (*brabeion*) of joy. To the fighter [Jacob]

---

14.   Philo employs both athletic and military imagery in allegorising Israel's battles.
15.   *On the Change of Names* 213; *Allegorical Interpretation* III, 193,13.

who through unabating and restless toils has made the good his own, his crown (*stephanos*) is the vision of God.[16]

With Philo there are heroic traits in God's athletes, but the ultimate goal and prize are not personal glory but the vision of God and the reception of divine blessings. Not long after Philo, another (unknown) Jewish writer pulled out all the stops in singing the praises of more recent athletes of God who were truly heroic.

The Maccabean martyr-athletes

Fourth Maccabees, a Jewish diatribal homily written in Greek,[17] betrays its debt to contemporary Hellenistic philosophy with its recurring theme: 'Pious reason rules supreme over the passions'. Here, not the natural reason of the Stoics but only devout, God-fearing reason can control one's sensibilities; that is, reason as directed by the divine law. Now it is the noble Maccabean martyrs who are the true champions of virtue as they wrestle against the evil antagonist, the Syrian Antiochus Epiphanes IV who desecrated the Jerusalem temple with pig's blood and carried out an horrific pogrom against the faithful who resisted his hellenisation program. Not the pagan sage but the Jewish martyr is the *true* athlete. In Fourth Maccabees, the old man Eleazar and the mother with her seven sons, who endure excruciating torture when called to renounce the God of Israel, perform greater toils than Hercules ever endured.[18]

A few passages will suffice to show how the athletic metaphor dominates the entire account of the pious martyrs. Eleazar 'endured the toils . . . and like a noble athlete being buffeted, conquered his tormenters' (4 Maccabees 6:9, 10). Defying the tyrant's threats, the seven brothers cry out, 'We through our evil treatment and endurance will win the prizes of virtue and be with God, for whom we suffer' (9:8). As in the Cynic-Stoic diatribe, athletic and military images flow into each other, as when

---

16. *On Rewards and Punishments* 27.
17. The exact time and location of writing is unknown but Antioch in the first century CE is a reasonable guess.
18. See 4 Maccabees 9:17, 18; 11:25; 15:11–13. For a fuller treatment of the relevant material in 4 Maccabees and other Hellenistic Jewish sources, including the Testaments of the Twelve Patriarchs, 4 Ezra, and the writings of Josephus, see Pfitzner, *Paul and the Agon Motif*, 57–72.

the first brother, dying in the flames, cries out to the others, 'Imitate me, my brothers. Do not desert me in my contest . . . Fight a holy and honourable warfare on behalf of righteousness' (9;23, 24). Just as athletic heroes were once feted at Olympia and the other national games, so now the victorious Jewish martyrs are acclaimed as true 'champions of virtue' (12:16), as God's athletes who have carried off the true prize (15:29; 16:14, 16). In 17:11–16 there appears an epitaph that reads like a Pindaric ode dedicated to the champions:

> For truly it was a holy contest that they contested. For on that day virtue, putting them to the test through endurance set before them the prize of victory: incorruption in everlasting life. The first to contest was Eleazar; the mother of the seven sons also joined in the contest, and the sons also contested. The tyrant was their antagonist and the world and all humanity were the spectators. Godliness won the victory, crowning her athletes. Who but wondered at the athletes of the divine law? Who were not amazed at them? (my translation)

Here, as we shall presently see, are the beginnings of the standard vocabulary of the later Christian martyr acts.

Paul and his co-workers as athletes of Christ

It is unlikely that Paul, or many of his readers for that matter, had first-hand experience of athletic contests. His strict Pharisaic upbringing would have made him averse to watching men competing naked (public contests and gymnastic exercises were male affairs back then), quite apart from the religious connotations of athletic contests. His timetable hardly left time for sitting in the stands, barracking for the local favourites. (Only one site of the national games, Isthmia, was close to a Pauline base of operations, Corinth.) In any case, Paul the traveller was always more likely to become a gladiatorial victim than a heroic contestant!

It has long been recognised that Paul's use of athletic imagery has more to do with language that was 'in the air' than with personal experience and powers of observation; his use clearly presupposes the long tradition of images and terms from the games in both pagan philosophy and Hellenistic Judaism. That his home town, of Tarsus in Cilicia, was a Stoic centre helps to explain this and other echoes of the Stoics and Cynics in Paul's letters.[19] Traditional features are clear in the best known example of the apostle's agonistic imagery:

> You know, of course, that all those running in a stadium compete, but only one gets the prize. Run in such a way that you gain it. Every competing athlete practices total self-control. They do it to gain a perishable victor's wreath; we do it to gain one that is imperishable. So then, I don't run without a clear goal; when boxing, I make my punches count. Indeed, I practice a punishing self-discipline lest, having proclaimed to others, I might be disqualified (1 Corinthians 9:24–27, own translation).

Carried over from the popular moral diatribes is the theme of self-discipline in the pursuit of a noble goal, the contrast between perishable and imperishable prizes, the multiplication of images, and the opening rhetorical litotes: 'Do you not know . . . ?' But this is no piece of popular moral philosophy merely espousing achievement by effort. It is highly unlikely that the apostle of grace would here reject what he otherwise insisted on, namely, that 'what counts is not what human beings want or try to do (literally, *run* to do), but the mercy of God' (Romans 9:16, JB). But the apostle also knew that grace calls and equips its recipients for hard work! The image of the striving athlete implies intense effort and application of all one's energies, but Paul's main focus is always on the goal of Christian striving.

First Corinthians 9:24–27 is set in a discussion on whether the Christian is free to eat meat dedicated to an idol. Paul's answer recalls the Hellenistic philosophers' quest for freedom, but it is startlingly different. A person is free only when able to give up freedom for the good of others. As the beginning of First Corinthians 9 shows, Paul is using his own behaviour as an apostle to illustrate how true freedom works. It means self-control to the point of self-renunciation in order to

---

19.   An excellent early example of study in Paul's indebtedness to diatribal rhetoric
       is Rudolf Bultmann's dissertation, *Der Stil der paulinischen Predigt und die kynisch-*
       stoische Diatribe (Göttingen: Vandenhoeck & Rupprecht, 1910).

become all things to all people (vv 19–23). Paul here represents a break in the tradition of athletic imagery in the sense that the context is no longer merely a personal ethic but the apostle's struggle for the free course of the gospel. Nothing is to impede the course of the gospel, not even Paul's own rights and freedoms—thus his repeated concern that he has not 'run in vain' (Galatians 2:2; Philippians 2:16).

St Paul also uses the image of the runner to picture the life of faith in eschatological perspective. He cannot yet claim perfection in the crucified and risen Lord, but

> I press on to make it my own, because Christ Jesus has made me his own; but this one thing I do: forgetting what lies behind and straining to what lies ahead, I press on toward the goal for the prize of the heavenly call of God in Jesus Christ. (Philippians 2:12–14)

Even where athletic terminology is used without development of a full metaphor, it expresses similar concerns for the unhindered effectiveness of the gospel message, despite all opposition to it, as an eschatological goal.[20] Suffering may be involved in this 'contest', but there is a complete absence of any heroics. The Stoic sage, contesting for equanimity against the blows of fate and feeling, can see himself as a spectacle to gladden the hearts of gods and human beings.[21] From a purely formal point of view, Paul's use of the image is similar: 'I think that God has exhibited us apostles as . . . a spectacle to the world, to angels and to human beings' (1 Corinthians 4:9). But whereas the Stoic moral athlete is to be seen as a source of wonderment and admiration, Paul sees himself and his co-workers in their contest of suffering for the gospel's sake, as human scum, sentenced to death. They march in Christ's triumphal procession, not their own (2 Corinthians 2:14). Self-glorification is ruled out; human

---

20.   As in Rom 15:30 ('strive together with me in your prayers . . . that I may be delivered . . .'), Phil 1:27 ('with one mind striving side by side for the faith of the gospel'), Phil 4:3 ('they have striven side by side with me in the gospel'). See also Col 1:29–2:1 (Paul's striving to present Christ) and 1 Thess 2:2 (he has presented the gospel with much struggle [Greek, *agon*]). The wrestling in Ephes 2:12 is part of an extended military metaphor.

21.   See Seneca *On Providence* 2,7–12, Epictetus *Dissertations* II 19,25 and III 22,59.

weakness is the arena in which God's power is exhibited (2 Corinthians 4:7–12).

By the time we reach the so-called Pastoral Letters, the picture of the athlete has become standard in referring to the apostle and those who are to carry on the apostolic mission. Timothy is encouraged to 'fight the good fight (*agon*) of faith' (1 Timothy 6:12), being prepared to suffer as a good soldier of Christ, for 'an athlete is not crowned unless he competes according to the rules' (2 Timothy 2:3–5). Since opposition to the gospel is part of the contest, athletic and military images become interchangeable.[22] The final word is given to the apostolic athlete and warrior *par excellence*:

> I have fought the good fight [contest], I have finished the race, I have kept the faith. From now on there is reserved for me the crown of righteousness, which the Lord, the righteous judge, will give me on that day, and not only to me but also to all who have longed for his appearing. (2 Timothy 4:7, 8, *NRSV*)

There are further echoes of Paul's picture of the athlete of the gospel in the letters of Ignatius of Antioch, especially in his letter to Polycarp. The fellow-bishop is exhorted to press on as he runs his 'course' with the grace given to him, and to 'bear the sicknesses of all as a perfect athlete. Where the toil is greatest, the gain is great' (Polycarp 1:2, 3). He is to be 'sober as God's athlete' in order to gain the prize of immortality and eternal life (2:3; 3:1). All who hold office in the church are to 'contend together, run together, suffer together . . .' (6:1). The picture of the apostle as athlete striving and suffering for Christ reaches its fullest development in the apocryphal Acts of the Apostles. In the *Acts of Thomas* Christ is himself called 'our true and unbeatable athlete' who comes to the aid of his apostles as they engage in their own contests.[23]

---

22. 'The good warfare' in 1 Tim 1:18 equals 'the good contest' in 1 Tim 6:12 and 2 Tim 4:7.
23. For references in the Apocryphal Acts, also to the suffering of the noble Perpetua, an 'invincible athlete', see Pfitzner, *Agon Motif*, 199.

The Christian martyr-athletes[24]

As noted above, the call for readiness to suffer pain as an athlete in a metaphorical sense has a long history. Stoic sage, Maccabean martyr, Christian apostle—all endure pain because their contest involves an opponent, whether internal or external. Roots of a specifically Christian martyr tradition expressed in athletic imagery begin with the letter to the Hebrews. Here the struggles of the addressees to maintain the faith in the face of opposition are pictured as a contest to be endured with patience. Their 'hard struggle' (Greek, *athlesis*) in the past involved public abuse, imprisonment and loss of property (Hebrews 10:32-34). Facing the possibility of similar threats to faith in the future, they are to throw off the dead weight of sin and 'run with perseverance the race that is set before' them (12:1, 12, 13). We cannot yet speak of martyrdom in the technical sense since those addressed have not yet 'agonised' to the point of shedding blood (12:4). The witnesses (Greek, *martyres*) in 12:1 are those who, like the saints listed in chapter 11, have lived by persevering faith and run the race of endurance to its victorious conclusion.[25]

There are obvious echoes of Stoic imagery and a continuation of the Jewish martyr tradition in the picture of the death of Peter and Paul in *First Clement* 5 and 6.

> Let us come to those who became athletes in the days nearest to us. Let us take the noble example of our own generation. Because of jealousy and envy the greatest and most righteous pillars of the church were persecuted . . . and contended until death.

The writer goes on to picture the trials of the apostles, including the journeys of Paul in the East and to the West, and his winning of the prize for endurance. There is no concentration on the excruciating agonies the apostles suffered. The apostolic martyrs are put forward as models of faithful endurance, just as the Stoics pointed to a demythologised

24.   What follows comes from my article, 'Martyr and Hero: the Origin and Development of a Tradition in the Early Christian Martyr Acts', in *Lutheran Theological Journal* 15:1,2 (May-August 1981): 9–17.
25.   There are only hints at the Jewish martyr tradition; compare Heb 11:35, 36 with 2 Macc 6:19, 28.

Hercules as a paragon of virtue. Paul's labours and travels recall the figure of the Stoic sage who is prepared to wander far and wide in search of virtue. In the final analysis, however, the account in First Clement remains closer to that of the martyrs in 4 Maccabees with its picture of the contest to the point of death, and closer to the Pauline and deutero-Pauline picture of the good fight of faith than to the Stoic picture of the moral contest of the philosopher.

The *Martyrdom of Polycarp* provides the first example of a new literary genre in the early church, the martyr-acts. And for the first time the athletic image becomes part of the standard language of martyrdom; the faithful witness to Christ in death has become *the athlete*. We gain an insight into the purpose of this fascinating document from 18:3: Polycarp's ashes are preserved 'to commemorate those who have already contested and to prepare those who are still to suffer'. As in 4 Maccabees, the noble and holy contest of martyrdom is fought against a godless tyrant who does at least show some respect for the age of the martyr. In both documents the tormenters waver in their purpose, the fires are cold for the martyrs, and spectators marvel at the heroic endurance of the sufferers. [26]

Only when the traditional character of the athletic image is appreciated can its continued retention in the martyr-acts be understood—after all, the contests of the gladiatorial arena had nothing in common with the athletic contests of ancient Greece. If there is any polemic against other athletes, it is no longer directed against those participating in physical games but against other 'athletes', using the term in a figurative sense. But any claim to superiority over the Jewish martyrs is never even implied for the simple reason that the early church adopted them as its own![27]

That a standard imagery remained firmly embedded in the Christian martyrologies down to the fourth century can easily be documented from the writings of such Fathers as Tertullian, Origen and Augustine. The peak of this development is seen in the *Church History* of Eusebius, and particularly in his account of the *Palestinian Martyrs*. Once more the contest is holy. It is fought against the earthly ruler as against Satan

---

26. See Pfitzner, 'Martyr and Hero', 14 for documentation of parallel features in the two documents

27. See Eduard Lohse, *Märtyrer und Gottesknecht* (Göttingen: Vandenhoeck & Rupprecht, 1963), 72.

himself. Once more the martyrs are given the heroic epithet 'noble'; again they strive for an immortal prize.[28] So tenacious was the traditional language that it was easily transferred into the Latin language. Tertullian even gives us the far-fetched image of the Father as the heavenly promoter of the contest, the Holy Spirit as the trainer, and the Son as the referee![29]

The ascetic athlete

Running parallel to the portrayal of the martyr as athlete was the depiction of the eremite as God's athlete. This ascetic contest can be documented as early as *Second Clement* 7 where the struggle against the flesh to keep the seal of baptism pure and undefiled is portrayed in a way that brings us closer to the Stoic diatribes and Philo than to Paul and the acts of the martyrs—though the contest of the ascetic and martyr can merge, as in the apocryphal *Martyrdom of Matthew* (2) or the *Sibylline Oracles* (II 48, 49). The growth of eremitic and monastic ideals naturally furthered the concept of an ascetic contest. An excellent example of this can be seen in Syriac literature, in the seventh treatise of Aphraates, the Persian, in *Concerning the Penitents*. Here the candidate for baptism is called to a contest (Syriac, *aguna*) of asceticism, with baptism itself called the water of testing. 'He who has purified his soul is fit for the contest, because he no longer has anything behind him which he could remember or to which he could again relapse'.[30]

In the psalms of Manichean Gnosticism there is virtually a return to the anthropological dualism presupposed in the Stoic portrayal of the moral athlete fighting against the passions of the flesh. Thus we find the following heroic acclamation: 'All hail, o busy soul that has finished her fight (*agon*) and subdued the ruling power, the body and its affections. Receive the garland from the hand of the Judge'.[31] As also in *Pistis Sophia* (249), the goal of the 'athlete' is the suppression of physical desires in the effort to escape physical restrictions and to preserve the divine spark implanted in the soul. The hero is once more the moral athlete. In tracing a trajectory we have returned to our starting point in a long tradition!

---

28. See the Church History V 1.17 and 36; VIII 2.3, 7.2, Palestinian Martyrs III, IV 4 and VIII 13.
29. See his *To the Martyrs* 3.
30. Text in *Patrologia Syriaca I*, edited by J Parisot (Paris, 1894, cols. 341-350).
31. *A Manichaean Psalm Book*, edited by C R A Allberry (Stuttgart, 1938), 57.

We are the champions?

We have here offered only a brief summary of a long trajectory, noting common themes and changing emphases. There are elements of the traditional metaphor that do not sit well with us today. For example, the anthropological dualism presupposed in classical Greek and Hellenistic images of the true athlete of the gods in the quest for self-control and piety does not rhyme with our unitary understanding of the human person. Furthermore, there is a pronounced individualism in the ancient philosophical picture of the champion of the gods; it leads to heroics, to a glorifying of the individual who makes it! The temptation to seek glory in martyrdom is not unknown in the Christian story, but those who have shed their blood in genuine witness to the truth have done so to God's glory, not their own.

This is not to say that sporting imagery has no place in modern Christian rhetoric—apart from the obligatory attention seeking mention of a local team's success or failure in the Sunday sermon! The imagery of St Paul and other New Testament writers still speaks to people in a world that loves sports. But the faithful are more likely to tune into sporting illustrations that highlight the need for teamwork, self-discipline and perseverance, rather than glorifying the spirit of competition and individual winners.

That the faithful will finally receive the reward of a crown at the end of their 'race' is a common theme of New Testament writers.[32] But any claim to be victorious champions of faith has a hollow ring these days. Whom are we trying to defeat? In the aftermath of the Christian crusades, medieval and modern, in light of a militant Christian Right that supports a war against terror that only increases the terrors of war, and in the shadow of fanatical Muslim fundamentalism that calls mass murderers martyrs, all heroic posturing and rocket-rattling in the name of religion is blasphemous and verges on the obscene.

The military image has almost squeezed out the athletic in popular expressions of Christian piety. 'Fight the good fight with all thy might' is, for many, a clearer call to action than 'Run the straight race through God's good grace'! But it has become increasingly hard to sing some of the old spiritual warfare hymns, which call on the soldiers of the cross

---

32. See 1 Cor 9:25; 2 Tim 4:8; James 1:12; 1 Peter 5:4; Rev 2:10; 3:11.

to stand up and fight for Jesus. They smell of a triumphalism that has all too often reared its ugly head in the history of the church.

Christianity has its champions, but they don't always look like winners, including modern saints like Dietrich Bonhoeffer and Mother Theresa. It's the meek who will inherit the earth and it's perhaps the host of little suffering servants who will make the greatest impact in our world. We are not called on to be winners but to claim the one victory that makes us all 'more than conquerors' (Romans 9:37). Perhaps it's the motif of competition with others ending in adulation for the winner that most holds us back from modern adaptations of an ancient and long standing image. A true athlete of Christ in the marathon of faith would surely stop to pick up the weary and fallen to help them across the line!

Meanwhile we will thank God for games, admire the champions, and enjoy our sports whether as competitors or as supporters in the stands and on the couch—without, hopefully, falling into the trap of making sport our idol.

Chapter Four

Sport, Femininity And The Promises Of The Theology Of The Body[1]

Synthia Sydnor

This is an essay about the possibility of studying issues related to sport and femininity in terms of Christian thought and thereby also of gaining a critical understanding of the cultural context of contemporary sport studies. In Christian theology, humans are members of the mystical body of Christ. This membership is a mystical embodiment, a graced existence on earth that connects one to God, eternity, heaven, angels, the communion of Saints. How does the study of femininity and sport fit into this and why should we care?

My writing here has these purposes: I mean to outline a rationale for taking such a topic seriously and also, in doing so, I briefly attempt to sample and document how academic research (and also popular culture) in the past twenty years or so regarding 'femininity and sport' has rarely included a Christian philosophical rendering of these issues. Further development of this thought may serve to enrich and positively change the phenomenological and ontological possibilities and forms of future sport. Although this work may be somewhat unique because it considers the case of sport, it is important to point out that there is much superb deliberation in the past decade that sets forth initiatives about a new kind of feminism in Christ.[2]

1. I thank Rob Hess and Gordon Preece for their interest in my work and for their constructive editorial comments. I also extend my sincere appreciation to an anonymous reviewer, whose extensive comments provided me with insight on rethinking and refining my project. For Rev Fr Dwight Campbell and Adria Olmi, OPB: thank you, more than words can say, for nurturing my interest in this topic and for your bibliographic contributions.
2. For example, Linda Woodhead, 'Spiritualising the Sacred: A Critique of Feminist Theology', in *Modern Theology*, 13/2 (April 1997), 193–194; Tina Beattie, *New Catholic*

Scholarship that specifically addresses religion and women's sport usually centers on understanding secularization within the context of athletes and religious fundamentalism (for example, women's sports participation in Muslim countries[3]) or on historical discourses of Muscular Christianity.[4] Hundreds of studies, typified by pioneering works such as that of Pat Griffin's *Strong Women, Deep Closets: Lesbians and Homophobia in Sport,* also uncover the history of discrimination and harmful prejudice against women (whatever their sexual orientation) involved in sport. Mainstream research approaches to questions surrounding gender and sport are dominated by ideas that stereotypical femininity is oppressive to women in sport, and if religion is considered in gender / sport studies, Christianity itself is usually depicted as naïve and repressive, a religion at odds with sophisticated critical studies of sport.[5] For example, when I

Feminism: Theology and Theory (New York: Routledge, 2006); Michele M Schumacher, editor, *Women in Christ: Toward a New Feminism* (Grand Rapids: Eerdmans, 2004); Ronda D Chervin, *Feminine, Free and Faithful* (Steubenville OH: Franciscan University Press, 1995); Léonie Caldecott, 'Sincere Gift: The New Feminism of John Paul II', in William Oddie, editor, *John Paul the Great: Maker of the Post-Conciliar Church* (San Francisco: Ignatius Press, 2005), 109–130.

3.   For example K Walseth and Kari Fasting, 'Islam's View on Physical Activity and Sport: Egyptian Women Interpreting Islam', in *International Review for the Sociology of Sport,* 38/1 (2003), 45–61; J Afary, 'The War Against Feminism in the Name of the Almighty: Making Sense of Gender and Muslim Fundamentalism', in *New Left Review,* 24 (July/August 1997), 1–21.

4.   For the most part, studies of religion and sport, attend to standpoint epistemologies and ethnography mostly surrounding evangelical Protestantism (for example, studies of church youth club sports participants, evangelical Christian professional athletes' lives, or the challenges of 'traditional' [Christian] ideologies by contemporary physical education students. For example Doune Macdonald and David Kirk, 'Pedagogy, the Body and Christian Identity', in *Sport, Education & Society;* 4/2 (1999), 131–142; Paul Carpenter, 'The Importance of a Church Youth Club's Sport Provision to Continued Church Involvement', in *Journal of Sport & Social Issues,* 25/3 (2001), 282–300; Ken Baker, 'Jock Evangelism: Defining and Degrading American Christianity for Future Generations,' in Ray Broadus Browne, Marshall William Fishwick, editors, *Preview 2001+: Popular Culture Studies in the Future* (Madison, WI: Popular Press, 1995), 189–206; Gary Land, 'God and the Diamond: The Born-Again Baseball Autobiography', in Edward J Rielly, editor, *Baseball and American Culture* (Binghamton, NY: Hayworth Press, 2001), 239–248.

5.   Griffin, *Strong Women, Deep Closets, op cit,* 109–132, includes a chapter 'We Prey, They Pray? Lesbians and Evangelicals in Sport'.

presented earlier versions of this work at an international sport studies conference, the audience focused not on the particulars of my paper, but solely on engaging me to defend the international scandal involving Catholic priests' sexual abuse of minors and/or (as perceived by my colleagues) the Catholic Church's historical hierarchy/ideologies of power. I answered that beyond the human failures and historical wrongs of the Catholic Church, there is an astonishing, rich, theological tradition from which we can begin to ask 'fresh'[6] questions of sport, feminism and gender.

Throughout this essay, as I just did, I also interweave some of my personal insight on how I came to this topic and on how my preliminary attempts to integrate this work into the secular academy have been received. I usually identify as a scholar neither of contemporary sport nor gender studies; rather, being trained in an interdisciplinary program in the humanities, I label myself as a historian-anthropologist of play.

While the majority of contemporary work on theology and gender construes Christianity as 'a set of dogmas that suppress imagination and individual creativity, distrust sex and the body, and systematically deprive women of power',[7] Linda Woodhead and Tina Beattie's extensive critiques about Christianity and feminism are more allied to my current project. Woodhead censures feminist theology for ignoring 'more complex realities of the Christian faith, past and present, by a preference for a rather simplistic modern construal of Christianity,' and for shunning 'attentive engagement with Christian tradition, scripture, and community in favour of the higher authority named 'women's experience' or 'women's discourses'. Woodhead instead tries to develop a Christian theology of the open, transcendant possibilities of gender identity, an identity 'bound up with my wider graced existence as a member of the body of Christ'.[8]

---

6.   Holly Thorpe, 'Foucault, Technologies of Self, and the Media: Discourses of Femininity in Snowboarding Culture', in *Journal of Sport & Social Issues,* 32 (May 2008), 224–225, uses the phrase 'fresh questions' (from leading feminist sport scholar CL Cole).

7.   Paraphrased from Woodhead, 'Spiritualising the Sacred,' *op cit,* 193–194.

8.   *Ibid,* 191–192. Woodhead also criticizes 'the stranded account of modern selfhood'; and points out in other work that 'holistic spiritualities and health practices are both self-centered and concerned with self-fulfillment of a distinctly sensuous kind'. Both of these critiques are valuable lines to pursue in regard to women and

In her 2006 book, Beattie concentrates on laying out a creative view
of Catholic feminism informed by Hans Urs von Balthasar. In so doing,
she builds upon her earlier work that looked at how John Paul II and
Luce Irigaray's ideas about women—although seemingly unlikely—are
complementary in that both Irigaray and John Paul call for ways for
women to be realized in society as uniquely themselves, not framed
according to males.[9] Irigaray seeks a new language and symbolism
which would allow women to 'be spoken by and for herself for the first
time'[10]—and Beattie believes that this language and symbolism is to be
found in Christian theology, long ignored by feminists:

> for the question of anthropology [of woman/women]
> hinges on the question of theology (even or especially *in
> absentia*—resistance to theology is a subliminal but potent
> influence on feminist theory) which brings back into focus
> the question of the relationship of women to God which
> is inseparable from the elusive question of being itself.
> For notwithstanding feminism's resistance to questions of
> theology and faith, the theoretical discourses that position
> postmodern feminism are haunted by the question of
> God.[11]

In the same way that Woodhead and Beattie are critical of feminist
theorists, within the slighter realm of sport studies, I too have been
disappointed in critical/cultural and feminist theorists' failure to
wrestle with Christian theology in a serious way. I believe that we can
use John Paul II and others such as Edith Stein, Michel de Certeau and
Graham Ward to revitalize how we envision embodiment, philosophy of
difference, and sport itself. In this present essay I introduce John Paul II's

sport. See Eva Sointu and Linda Woodhead, 'Spirituality, Gender, and Expressive
Selfhood', in *Journal for the Scientific Study of Religion*, 47/2 (May 2008), 272.

9.   Tina Beattie, 'Carnal Love and Spiritual Imagination: Can Luce Irigaray and John
     Paul II Come Together?', in Jon Davies and Gerard Loughlin, editors, *Sex These
     Days: Essays on Theology, Sexuality and Society* (Sheffield: Sheffield Academic Press,
     1997), 160–183.

10. Davies and Loughlin, *Sex These Days, op cit*, 11.

11. Beattie, *New Catholic Feminism*, 35.

phenomenology about the body as a framework that provides us with philosophical undergirding to do better with gender, sport and religion studies. After becoming a Roman Catholic and studying Pope John Paul II's 'theology of the body' I found much of what I learned applicable to the study of sport: there is a body of thought that poses a challenge to sociological, historical and cultural literature about femininity and sport and so here, I assess how John Paul II's teachings may lend to conversations about sport an intellectual fullness.

As is often described, the Pope was an athlete, enjoying soccer, skiing and hiking and an active outdoor life. On the eve of the 2004 Athens Summer Olympic Games, he established the Pontifical Council of the Laity—Church and Sports (in July 2008 the organization became the John Paul II Foundation for Sports). This foundation has as its aim the interpretation of sport in light of Christianity and our present cultural moment.[12]

Building on the reflections of his earlier predecessors,[13] over the three decades of his pontificate, John Paul commented on sport in some 120 addresses, speeches and messages in which I identify several overlapping themes:

- Sport's role in building a more united and peaceful world;[14]
- Sport's missionary purpose;[15]

---

12. 'Bishop: John Paul II Knew Role of Sports: Vatican Launches Foundation to Promote Values', accessed at Zenit.org http://www.zenit.org/article-23361?l=english on 28 July 2008.

13. Pius XI, *Non Abbiamo Bisogno, Encyclical on Catholic Action in Italy*, 22, June 29, 1931 accessed at http//www.vatican.va/holy_father/pius_xi/encyclicals/d on 1 June 2004; *Mit Brennender Sorge, Encyclical on the Church and the German Reich*,34, May 14, 1937 accessed at http//www.vatican.va/holy_father/pius_xi/encyclicals/d on 19 July 2004; Pius XII *Invicti Athletae, Encyclical on St. Andrew Bobola*, May 16, 1957, accessed at http://www.vatican.va/holy_father/pius_xii/encyclicals/ on 19 July 2004.

14. For example 'Message of John Paul II to the Athletes, Politicians and Dignitaries of Italian, Israeli and Palestinian Culture Taking Part in the "Match of the Heart"', 25 May 2000 accessed at http://www.vatican.va/holy_father/john_paul_ii/speeche on 19 July 2004; *Consecrated Persons and Their Missions in Schools: Reflections and Guidelines* II.79, Oct. 28, 2002 accessed at http://www.vatican.va/roman_curia/congregations/ccath on 19 July 2004.

15. For example, 'Children have a special bond with the Virgin Mary,' John Paul II's

- Sport's role in the harmonious development of body and mind;[16]
- Sport's spiritual characteristics;[17]
- the dark side of the sports world;[18]
- the ethical dimensions of entertainment and new and emerging media;[19]
- and for the purposes of this essay, an understanding of the place of culture in sport.

In my reading, it is in his later thought, (though not in much quantity), that the Pope comes to elaborate a bit on sport in regard to his anthropology of the human person—sport as a phenomenon with potential to contribute to the formative and full development of the individual and in a global dimension, to establishing 'the new civilization of love'.[20] In what he did say specifically about sport, John Paul II comes to have a sophisticated understanding of sport as possessing cultural, transformational qualities. For instance, listen to his 2000 homily on the Jubilee of Sports Persons: 'In recent years, [sport] has continued to grow even more as one of the characteristic phenomena of the modern era, almost a "sign of the times" capable of interpreting humanity's new needs and expectations'.[21] And in 2004, John Paul II envisions sports and tourism as 'two living forces for mutual understanding, culture and the

---

address to the young people of the Italian Catholic Action, Dec. 21, 2002 accessed at http://www.vatican.va/roman_curia/congregations/cevan on 19 June 2004.

16. For example, 'Address of John Paul II to the Managers, Players and Supporters of the Roma Sports Association' Nov. 30, 2000 accessed at http://www.vatican.va/holy_father/john_paul_ii/speeche on 15 July 2004.

17. For example 'Address of the Holy Father to the Organizers and Participants in the 83rd Giro D'Italia Cycle Race', May 12 2000 accessed at http://www.vatican.va/holy_father/john_paul_ii/speeche on /16 July 2004; 'Jubilee of Sports People,' *Homily of John Paul II* Oct. 29 2000 accessed at http://www.vatican.va/holy_father/john_paul_ii/homilies on 15 July 2004.

18. For example, 'Pope Cautions About the Dark Side of Sports World', *Zenit*, 7 Aug. 2004, http:www.zenit.org/.

19. For example, Pontifical Council for Social Communications, *Ethics in Communications* June 2, 2000 accessed at http://www.vatican.va.roman_curia/pontifical_councils/ on 15 September 2006.

20. Jubilee of Sports Persons, *Homily of John Paul II*, 29 October 2000.

21. Jubilee of Sports Persons, *Homily of John Paul II*, 29 October 2000.

development of societies'.[22] John Paul II's insights and perspectives on sport (such as those I just mentioned), albeit never gathered together in a single work or letter,[23] nevertheless help articulate a cohesive, significant understanding of modern humans' relationships to sport and play. Over his pontificate, beyond his direct notice and words about sport to those audiences in and with sport-related venues and purpose, the Pope also leaves us with an epistemological/ontological legacy for understanding a topic that he never actually mentioned: women and sport. I consider especially that John Paul II's large body of thought that is referred to as his 'theology of the body' has potential to be applied to conversing about what are seen as paradoxes and dilemmas in sport studies concerning gender, femininity and the culture of sport.

My evidence about the body that we can apply to the study of sport also comes from papal teachings contained in 129 general audience talks given by John Paul II between 1979 and 1984 that have been compiled into separate books. In addition, the writings of John Paul II in *On the Dignity and Vocation of Women* (1988); *The Gospel of Life* (1995); and *The Splendor of Truth* (1993) are considered as these are often grouped with John Paul's 'theology of the body' works. My discussion highlights the following notions emphasised by John Paul II's works as central to critiquing contemporary ideas of femininity and the culture of sport: First, there is Mary as a model for humanity. Pope John Paul II's Mariology puts forward that the human body becomes glorious by doing the will of God as Mary did when she gave her *fiat* to the angel bearing news that she would conceive the Son of God. Mary is 'not an archetypal feminine, but herself a "poor woman of mud and clay" who has the wisdom to live in obedience to God within the human condition'.[24] Second, there is the idea of the triune nature of humanity. This idea is rooted in the belief that dignity comes from union with God. As philosopher David L Schindler explains, 'the distinguishing feature of an adequate notion of person,

---

22. Message of John Paul II for the 25th World Day of Tourism, 27 September 2004.

23. An exception is Robert Feeney, *The Catholic Ideal: Exercise & Sports* (Fort Collins, CO: Ignatius Press, 2005) which calls itself 'a handy compendium of Catholic doctrine culled from the teaching of the Popes and offers excellent practical tips on the benefits of regular daily exercise', 11.

24. Rocco Buttiglione, *Karol Wojtyla: The Thought of the Man Who Became Pope John Paul II* (Grand Rapids: Eerdmans, 1997), 25.

finally is love: relation to God and to all other creatures in God'.[25] And thirdly, Pope John Paul II's theology of the body interrupts the dominant mode of doing gender and sport studies because it declares that female nature affords women distinct physical and spiritual capabilities with which to participate in the social order; John Paul calls this the 'genius' of woman.

I am an adult convert in 1998 to the Catholic faith, but I do not have a dramatic conversion story except to say that organised religion was the last thing I ever imagined myself doing. If I have to identify an intermediary in my half-century journey to Catholicism, perhaps I would identify disparate reading that somehow all at once made everything new: translating parts of the New Testament to practice ancient Greek; working on essays about writing and representation; coming across the first lines of the Catechism of the Catholic Church ('The desire for God is written in the human heart'[26]) and Michel de Certeau's 1971 lecture, 'How is Christianity Thinkable Today',[27] in which Certeau attempts to grasp the situation of Christianity in modernity. Christianity is a relationship to a past event—the event of Jesus Christ's death and resurrection—to which it must seek to be faithful. Certeau argues that the *form* of Jesus' death and resurrection is reproduced with different content in various experiences. It is something *said-between*,[28] which cannot be identified with any one particular practice, experience or concept, but which haunts the gaps between 'a multiplicity of practices and discourses which neither "preserve" nor "repeat" the event,'[29] yet which would not exist without it. Christianity, then, must always be thought of in such a way that it perpetually repeats the difference of its founding event, that it permits new 'spaces' in which Christianity is enacted.[30] After my entry

25. David L Schindler, 'Which Ontology is Necessary for an Adequate Anthropology', in *Anthropotes*, 15/2 (1999), 423.
26. *Catechism of the Catholic Church* (Ligouri, MO: Ligouri Publications, English translation, 1994), 1.27.
27. Michel de Certeau, 'How is Christianity Thinkable Today?' (translated by Frederick Christian Bauerschmidt and Catriona Hanley) in *The Postmodern God: A Theological Reader,* edited by Graham Ward (Malden, MA: Blackwell Publishers, 1997), 142–158 (reprinted from *Theology Digest*, 19 (1971), 334–345.
28. *Ibid*, 145.
29. *Ibid*, 146.
30. *Ibid*, 147.

into the Church, as I followed such intellectual trajectories in my career as a professor at the University of Illinois, I now tried to understand these in terms of Christianity, its enactment, and sports place in this'.[31]

While I felt that exploration of the melding of truth, reason, Christianity, and sport was legitimate,[32] there has continued to be debate in my sport studies circle (for example among those who are members of the North American Society for Sport History (NASSH); the North American Society for the Sociology of Sport (NASSS); the International Society for the History of Physical Education and Sport

---

31. See for example, Graham Ward, editor, *The Postmodern God: A Theological Reader* (Malden, MA and Oxford: Blackwell Press, 1997); Catherine Pickstock, *After Writing: On the Liturgical Consummation of Philosophy* (Oxford: Wiley Blackwell, 1998); John Milbank, Graham Ward, and Catherine Pickstock, editors, *Radical Orthodoxy* (London: Routledge 1999); Graham Ward, *Cities of God* (London: Routledge 2000); John Milbank and Catherine Pickstock, *Truth in Aquinas* (London: Routledge, 2001); Graham Ward, editor, *The Blackwell Companion to Postmodern Theology* (Oxford: Blackwell, 2001); Lewis Ayres and Gareth Jones, editors; *Christian Origins: Theology, Rhetoric and Community* (London: Routledge, 1998).

32. Some of the works that helped me integrate my professorate with Catholicism are John Milbank, *Theology and Social Theory: Beyond Secular Reason* (Oxford and Cambridge: Blackwell, 1990), 69, 79–87, 93, 97, 210–ff, 246–248; John Milbank, *Being Reconciled: Ontology and Pardon* (London: Routledge, 2003); Robert Sokolowski, *Eucharistic Presence: A Study in the Theology of Disclosure* (Washington DC: The Catholic University of America Press, 1994); Douglas J Davies, *Anthropology and Theology* (Oxford and New York: Berg, 2002); Tracey Rowland, *Culture and the Thomist Tradition: After Vatican II* (London: Routledge, 2003), 20–28, 36–50, 66, 71-77, 109; Erazim Kohák, *The Embers and the Stars: A Philosophical Inquiry into the Moral Sense of Nature* (Chicago: University of Chicago Press, 1984). I paraphrase cultural studies professor Elizabeth Fox-Genovese, 'A Conversion Story', in *First Things* (April 2000): 39 who came into the Catholic Church at about the same time as I, as she confides about the reputation of Christian scholars in the secular academy:
      an adult conversion to Catholicism is not an everyday experience in the American academy ... most secular academics seem to receive any profession of Christian faith with a vague sense of embarrassment. Adherence to Judaism or Islam is another matter, although why is not immediately self-evident . . . Perhaps they meet with greater tolerance because they are less familiar, perhaps because they do not carry Christianity's taint of having long figured as the religion of a male European elite that used its faith to cow others into submission . . . A vague nondenominational Christianity—or better yet, Unitarianism—may be acceptable, but Catholicism lies beyond the pale, not something that people 'like us' embrace.

(ISHPES) or those who might publish in *The Journal of Sport & Social Issues* or the *International Journal of the History of Sport*), about the value of my research. For instance, since in some of my publications I revealed the influence of my religious beliefs,[33] my work has been called 'naïve nonsense'.[34] Allen Guttmann, a Professor of English and American Studies at Amherst College, who I would identify as one of the ten most important modern writers on sport and culture,[35] relates in a 2008 essay published in the *International Journal of the History of Sport*:

> Nearly a decade ago, Sydnor sent me a manuscript in which she candidly discussed two events that had changed her life. One event was her conversion to postmodernism, which assured her that there is no such thing as absolute truth; the other event was her conversion to Roman Catholicism, whose doctrines she seems to have accepted as absolute truth. I read the manuscript and sent Sydnor my criticism. I suggested that the second conversion seemed rather like an apostasy from the first. Sydnor replied that she'd give the matter some thought. I take her contribution to [the book] *Deconstructing Sport History* to mean that she has given the

---

33. Alberto Savorano, 'Reflections of an Anglican', in *LitteraeCommunionis*, 4 (2007), 36.

34. Allen Guttmann, 'Review Essay: The Ludic and the Ludicrous', in *International Journal of the History of Sport*, 25/1 (2008): 111.

35. For example, Allen Guttmann, *From Ritual to Record: The Nature of Modern Sports* (New York: Columbia University Press, 1978); *The Games Must Go On: Avery Brundage and the Olympic Movement* (New York: Columbia University Press, 1984); *Sports Spectators* (New York: Columbia University Press, 1986); *A Whole New Ball Game: An Interpretation of American Sports* (Chapel Hill: University of North Carolina Press, 1988); Allen Guttmann, Donald G Kyle and Gary D Stark, editors, *Essays on Sport History and Sport Mythology* (College Station, TX: Texas A&M Press, 1990); *Women's Sports: A History* (New York: Columbia University Press, 1991); *Games and Empires: Modern Sports and Cultural Imperialism* (New York: Columbia University Press, 1994); *The Erotic in Sports* (New York: Columbia University Press, 1996); *The Olympics: A History of the Modern Games* (Champaign: University of Illinois Press, 2002); *Sports: The First Five Millennia* (Amherst: University of Massachusetts Press, 2004).

matter considerable thought and has failed to resolve the logical contradiction.[36]

Guttmann criticises me for writing in another of my essays:[37] 'the aim of sport history is 'revealing and honoring God . . . There is nothing left for us to do on earth except this.'   Guttmann declares 'I am mystified by Sydnor's argument. It may be that Sydnor wants her readers to be mystified. She writes approvingly of "mystical ways that move beyond the literal and historical." Guttmann goes on to attach Lucretius' 'so much harm has been done in the name of religion',[38] to my work.

I do not agree with Guttmann's presumptions. It is possible to be mystifying (although I did not intend to be so*) and* at the same time to search for truth—Edith Stein comes to mind as an exemplar of this approach to intellectual and holy life: 'She ceased to write principally as a philosopher. She most definitely continued to employ reason put in the service of truths, that, though very much applicable to the human sphere, came from a source that transcended that sphere'.[39]

Guttmann implies that faith may stand as a barrier to one's professional obligation to discover the truth. Yet, for me *the* truth revealed in Christianity—a law—sets before me in my university work a whole new universe, a tremendous way of seeing and understanding, an everyday joy, a freedom and potential to invent, to move beyond strict boundaries, to journey toward God. Tina Beattie reiterates: 'if modern Catholic

---

36. The chapter that Guttmann criticises is Synthia Sydnor, 'Contact with God, Body and Soul', in *Deconstructing Sport History: A Postmodern Analysis,* edited by Murray Phillips (Albany, NY: State University of New York Press, 2006).
37. Allen Guttmann, 'Review Essay: The Ludic and the Ludicrous,' *International Journal of the History of Sport,* 25/1 (2008), 106-107.
38. *Ibid,* 107 (quoting Sydnor, 'Contact with God, Body and Soul', *op cit,* 203, 115, 208).
39. See Edith Stein, *The Science of the Cross* (Washington DC: Institute of Carmelite Studies, 2002) as quoted in DQ McInerny, 'Edith Stein as Mystical Theologian,' *Fellowship of Catholic Scholars* (Fall 2004), 30. See also Josephine Koeppel, *Edith Stein: Philosopher and Mystic* (Scranton PA: University of Scranton Press, 2007); and these works by Stein (all published by Washington DC: ICS Publications with English translations): *Essays On Woman,* translated by Freda Mary Oben, 1996; *Humanities,* edited by Marianne Sawicki, translated by Mary Catherine Baseheart and Marianne Sawicki, 2000; *Finite and Eternal Being,* edited by L Gelber and Romaeus Leuven, translated by Kurt F Reinhardt, 2002; *Knowledge and Faith,* translated by Walter Redmond, 1993.

theology is an awesome and sometimes terrifying force for feminists to grapple with, it is also, I believe, an inexhaustibly rich source for feminist reflection and analysis, a source of *jouissance* as well as abjection'.[40]

Guttmann and others do not understand how postmodernism and religious beliefs can meld. Yet, there are established projects like Beattie's that understand postmodern and religious thought to be complementary. As well, Catherine Pickstock's *After Writing: On the Liturgical Consummation of Philosophy*,[41] and the whole of the radical orthodoxy series published by Routledge, use postmodern thought as an avenue to radically conceptualize the present-day world as God-given mystery.[42] Of course, we know that Guttmann's response is emblematic of an important critique that one encounters when working from Christian standpoint epistemologies, so thus I recounted its distinctive reasoning in this paper so as to try to address concerns that many readers unsympathetic to this standpoint might advance.

Studying the Catholic faith, John Paul II's body of writing on theology of the body, and works that emphasize the idea of body-and-soul as whole-person in the Christian understanding, changed how I understood body, culture, and sport studies. Above all, there is this thing 'sport,' a uniquely human (unknown to non-human/ animals) cultural formation, universal, wondrous –and yes- mystical. From wherever it arose—in the roots of play-as-civilisation as Johan Huizinga, Josef Pieper, Roger Caillois and Bernard Suits,[43] would have it (I agree),

40.   Beattie, *New Catholic Feminism, op cit,* 10.

41.   Catherine Pickstock, *After Writing: On the Liturgical Consummation of Philosophy* (Malden, MA: Blackwell Press, 1997).

42.   For example, *The Postmodern God: A Theological Reader,* edited by Graham Ward (Malden, MA and Oxford: Blackwell Publishers, 1997); Frederick Christian Bauersmith, 'Aesthetics: The Theological Sublime', in *Radical Orthodoxy,* edited by John Milbank, Ward Graham, and Catherine Pickstock (London and New York: Routledge), 1999, 201–219; Zygmunt Bauman, 'Postmodern Religion?', in Paul Heelas, editor (with the assistance of David Martin and Paul Morris), *Religion, Modernity and Postmodernity* (Oxford: Blackwell Publishers, 1998), 55–78; Edith Wyschogrod, 'Saintliness and Some Aporias of Postmodernism From *Saints and Postmodernism'* in Ward, *op cit,* 341-355.

43.   Johan Huizinga, *Homo Ludens: A Study of the Play Element in Culture* (New York: Beacon Press, 1955); Josef Pieper, *Leisure: The Basis of Culture* (New York: Pantheon Books, 1952); Roger Caillois. *Man, Play and Games.* Meyer Barash, trans. (Champaign IL: University of Illinois Press, 2001; originally published as *Les jeux et les hommes*

or in the throes of the Industrial Revolution (as many sport historians document) the free will gifted to us humans by God has allowed sports in amazing ubiquitous manifestations to endure, perplex, inspire. As with architecture, art, law, mathematics, and so on, that sport in some variation seems to be essential to humankind speaks to me of God's imprint upon it. Humans may have muddled sport with commercialism, doping, cheating, eating disorders, violence and the like, but still, sport is often something stunningly special.

Although the athletes, sports spectators and scholars in my everyday life would have sport be something very distant from their faith/religious beliefs, my argument utilises the simple premise that there does not exist a split between faith and daily life and more intricate ideas of embodiment and faith. Gender identity does not close or oppress the question of who a person is, but rather opens it. Many feminist sport theorists today are on to this idea that physical activity, sport and play may act as practices of freedom and may create new choices about body practices, but they still interpret this freedom in a particular philosophical way.[44] For example, Pirrko Markula's excellent work reinterprets Michel Foucault to understand that power (such as that of sport as a masculine domain) is not necessarily evil nor should it be pre-assigned as either 'oppressive' or 'liberating':

> If Foucault theorizes that power is not necessarily an evil, the researchers should not automatically assume that powerful individuals in sport manage their power unethically . . . Or to put it in Foucauldian terms, how do ordinary women athletes bend the dominating 'outside' into themselves so that they can actually see differently and be seen differently? . . . women within sport need to

---

[Paris: Librairie Gallimard, 1958]); Bernard Suits, *The Grasshopper: Games, Life and Utopia* (New York: Harper Collins: 1978); Clifford Geertz, 'Deep Play: Notes on the Balinese Cockfight,' in Geertz, *The Interpretation of Cultures* (New York: Basic Books, 1977), 412–454.

44. For example, Thorpe, 'Foucault, Technologies of Self, and the Media: Discourses of Femininity in Snowboarding Culture', *op cit;* Leslie Heywood, *Bodymakers: A Cultural Anatomy of Women's Body Building* (Rutgers: Rutgers University Press, 1998); Leslie Goldman, *Locker Room Diaries: The Naked Truth about Women, Body Image, and Re-imagining the 'Perfect' Body* (Cambridge, MASS: Da Capo Press, 2007).

begin to question the limits of their identities and here, I
believe, lies the ethical responsibility of the sport feminists.
. . we should strive to embody the characteristics of a
critically aware individual who questions the limitations
of discursive feminine identity . . . we need to be in the
fore front of provoking the critical inquiring reaction to
women's sport through active dialogue with the sport
world. As players in the sporting truth game, we need to
reflect on the limits of our own identities to problematize
the boundaries of discursive femininity. Only then can
we use our knowledge and our power positions ethically
to take responsibility for encouraging athletes, coaches,
and others involved in sport to engage in critical self-
reflection.[45]

While the above call for 'ethical responsibility' certainly speaks to
Christian sensibilities, there is in Markula and others no hint (beyond
Foucauldian critiques) of alternative philosophies that could help
institute such projects. Where then do we begin?

What is known as John Paul's 'theology of the body' includes papal
teachings contained in 129 general audience talks given between 1979
and 1984. First published as separate books,[46] the audiences were brought
together in a 1997 English publication by the Daughters of St Paul Press
that is divided into two major parts: 'Original Unity of Man and Woman'
and 'Life According to the Spirit'. In addition, the teaching of Pope John
Paul II in *On the Dignity and Vocation of Women* (1988 Apostolic Letter,
Mulieris Dignitatem); The Gospel of Life (1995 Encyclical Letter, *Evangelium
Vitae*); and *The Splendor of Truth* (1993 Encyclical Letter, *Veritatis Splendor*);
and Pope Paul VI's *Of Human Life* (1968 Encyclical Letter, *Humanae
Vitae*) are considered developments and applications of the theology of
the body. The vision of John Paul II, which is referred to by some as
a phenomenological personalism, centers on 'the human person in the

---

45. Pirkko Markula, 'The Technologies of the Self: Sport, Feminism, and Foucault',
    Sociology of Sport Journal, 20 (2003), 100–101, 105.
46. *Original Unity of Man and Woman; Blessed are the Poor of Heart; The Theology of Marriage
    and Celibacy; Reflections on Humanae Vitae.*

light of the mystery of Christ'.[47] Importantly, John Paul's teachings are Marian, with Mary in a unique role of maternal mediation in the Church and in the history of humankind.[48] In 1978, two months after his election as Supreme Pontiff, John Paul II put the words *Totus tuus* (all thine) and 'the concept of entrustment of the Church and himself to Mary, in the context of her motherhood of the Church'.[49]

Indeed, moving through John Paul's writings I came to a greater awareness of what the Blessed Virgin Mary means to all of us—whatever our beliefs. The Marian dimension of the Catholic faith, fascinating and complex, places Mary as a symbol 'not of a female body but of a collective entity which includes all that is human'.[50] John Paul II provides commentary on all interpersonal relations by using the analogy of the union of spouses:

> Christ has entered history and remains in it as the Bridegroom who 'has given himself.' 'To give' means 'to become a sincere gift' in the most complete and radical way: 'Greater love has no man than this' (*John* 15:13). According to this conception, *all human beings—both women and men—are called* through the Church, *to be the 'Bride' of Christ, the Redeemer of the world.* In this way 'being the bride,' and thus the 'feminine' element, becomes a symbol of all that is 'human,' according to the words of Paul: 'There is neither male nor female, for you are all *one* in Christ Jesus' (*Galatians* 3.28).[51] [italics original]

Reference to the Blessed Virgin Mary in connection with modern sport may seem outlandish, so allow me to issue some disclaimers. When I discuss radical Christian femininity and call for a alternative rendering of women in sport via understandings of the Blessed Virgin Mary, I

47 John S. Grabowski, 'Forward,' in *The Theology of the Body: Human Love in the Divine Plan* (Boston: Pauline Books & Media, 1997), 20.

48 Brendan Leahy, '*Totus Tuus*: The Mariology of John Paul II,' in Oddie, *John Paul the Great*, 2005, *op cit*, 69-93.

49 Campbell, 'Mary, Mother of the Church,' *op cit*, 12.

50 Beattie, *op cit*.

51. Apostolic Letter of John Paul II, *On the Dignity and Vocation of Women* (1988), 25.

am *not* calling for women to abandon sport, for a return to patriarchal sport, for gender inequity, for separatist female sport that exudes grace or silence;[52] nor is a plea for evangelization, for Christian athletes to be enthusiastic about their faith, a central tenet of my argument. When I use the word 'femininity' in this essay, I intend its meaning to be close to John Paul II's (femininity as a 'specific charism'[53]). Later in my essay when I push for a new frame of sport, I will try to give some preliminary examples of sport in the spirit of Christian feminism. What do I mean by this feminism?

Over his pontificate, John Paul II developed his teaching that Mary helps all the faithful 'to seek persistently the path to perfect unity of the body of Christ through unreserved fidelity to the spirit of truth and love'.[54] In the Pope's teachings, with Mary as the model for a new kind of feminism, women are all mothers, whether physical or spiritual. From John Paul II's Encyclical Letter, *On the Gospel of Life*:

> In transforming culture ... *women* occupy a place, in thought and action, which is unique and decisive . . . Women first learn and then teach others that human relations are authentic if they are open to accepting the other person: a person who is recognised and loved because of the dignity that comes from being a person and not from other considerations, such as usefulness, strength, intelligence, beauty or health. This is the fundamental contribution that the Church and humanity expect from women. And it is the indispensable prerequisite for an authentic cultural change.[55]

52. Such as the classic Jane Erskine Stuart, *The Education of Catholic Girls* (New York: Biblio Bazaar, 2007, originally published 1914).

53. Pope John Paul II, 'Message to World Union of Catholic Women's Organizations', *Zenit* (20 March 2001): '[women should transmit] the "genuine meaning of faith and apply it to all circumstances of life . . . Woman has a truly unique talent to communicate the Christian message in the family and the realms of work, study and leisure.'

54. `Pope John Paul II, Afternoon Address, June 7 1981, quoted in Dwight F Campbell, 'Mary, Mother of the Church', in *Homiletic & Pastoral Review*, November 2003, CIV/2, 15.

55. John Paul II, 1995 Encyclical Letter *The Gospel of Life* (*Evangelium Vitae*), 99.

In Catholic theology, men also are seen to be bearers of Christ and caregivers of humanity, and the whole of humanity is seen as bodily living as sacramental Bride to Christ, 'the Church is a person, a woman in relation to the male Christ . . . it transcends, but is analogous to the sexual relationship between husband and wife: it is a "suprasexual relationship". . . the Church as a whole is feminine, open and dependent on her Bridegroom.'[56] Thus in the case of sexual difference, far from dividing humanity, the Pope understands difference as intended to come together in a unity of love, a communion of persons,[57] in his words:

> every individual is made in the image of God . . . [and] cannot exist alone . . . only as a 'unity of the two', and therefore *in relation to another human person* . . . Being a person in the image and likeness of God thus also involves existing in a relationship in relation to the other 'I'.[58]

The Pope illuminates that it is 'a question of understanding the reasons for and the consequences of the Creator's decision that the human being should always and only exist as a woman or a man'.[59] This situation —that would be considered dark to most feminist sport scholars working today—is marked by profound hope for John Paul II. He develops and highlights in his vast writings the hope that the fullness of time will manifest the extraordinary dignity of the woman.[60] For John Paul, this is the power of the redemption of the body in which, although human history is flawed by original sin, the grace of Christ enables— gives the body the capacity for—the expression of the whole person. This is love as an extremely difficult realisation that something other than oneself is real and needy. For John Paul II, this reality is centered on the philosophical, anthropological and theological understanding of unity as having a multiform dimension—ethical and sacramental—that is, realised through (to use John Paul's words) 'not only the "body," but

---

56.   Beattie, *New Catholic Feminism, op cit*, 134–136.
57.   John S Grabowski, 'Forward', in *The Theology of the Body: Human Love in the Divine Plan* (Boston: Pauline Books & Media, 1997), 17.
58.   Apostolic Letter of John Paul II, *On the Dignity and Vocation of Women* (1988), 7.
59.   *Ibid*, I.1.
60.   *Ibid*, II.4.

also the "incarnate" communion of persons'[61] exemplified for John Paul
II by the Holy Trinity, the Father-Son-Holy Spirit.

In *The Splendor of Truth*, John Paul II emphasises this triune—Father–
Son-Holy Spirit nature of this mutual relationship: 'The Spirit of Jesus,
received by the humble and docile heart of the believer, brings about
the flourishing of . . . holiness amid the great variety of vocations,
gifts, responsibilities, conditions and life situations'.[62] Sport is one such
vocation, gift, and life situation to which we can apply John Paul's
contemplations.

John Paul II's theology of the body highlights the triune nature of
humanity. Dignity comes from union with God; Schindler's passage
quoted above ('the distinguishing feature of an adequate notion of
person, finally is love: relation to God and to all other creatures in God"[63])
is a pertinent explanation. But this love is not narcissistic or utilitarian.
In contrast to John Paul II's phenomenology of the Trinity and reliance
on divine revelation and sacred scripture, commonly those interested in
the study and interpretation of female athletes and girls and women in
sport work from the perspectives of feminist theories, cultural studies,
interpretive-interactionism, neo-Marxism and/or poststructuralism.[64]
For example, take some leading textbooks on the subject: a Routledge
anthology, *Gender and Physical Education: Contemporary Issues and Future
Directions* states its approach as

---

61. John Paul II, General Audience, November 7 1979, 'Meaning of Unity', 5.
62. Encyclical Letter of John Paul II, *The Splendor of Truth*, III. 108.
63. David Schindler, 'Which Ontology is Necessary for an Adequate Anthropology', in
      Anthropotes, 15/2 (1999), 423.
64. For example, Iris Marion Young, *Throwing Like a Girl and Other Essays in Feminist
      Philosophy and Social Theory* (Oxford: Oxford University Press, 2005); Elizabeth
      Grosz, *Volatile Bodies: Toward a Corporeal Feminism* (Bloomington, IN: Indiana
      University Press, 1994); Susan Birrell and CL Cole, *Women, Sport and Culture*
      (Champaign, IL: Human Kinetics, 1994); Allison Dewar, 'Sexual Oppression in
      Sport: Past, Present and Future Alternatives', in *Sport in Social Development*, edited
      by Alan G. Ingham and John W Loy (Champaign, IL: Human Kinetics, 1993);
      Jennifer Hargreaves, *Sporting Females: Critical Issues in the History and Sociology of
      Women's Sports* (London: Routledge, 1994); Richard Giulianotti, *Sport: A Critical
      Sociology* (Cambridge: Polity Press, 2005), 80–101; John Hughson, David Inglis, and
      Marcus Free, *The Uses of Sport: A Critical Study* (London: Routledge, 2005),138–158;
      Grant Jarvie, *Sport, Culture and Society* (London: Routledge, 2006), 309-312.

concepts and language of Marxism and of interpretive sociology . . . attention to structural issues . . . attention in particular to the ways in which learning and values are attributed to physical and social objects of the social world and on how structures of convention, action and identity are created and reproduced in schooling and physical education . . . integrated with the more liberating perspectives of feminism.[65]

And Jay Coakley, in his widely used text, *Sport in Society: Issues & Controversies*, explains in his opening chapter on 'Gender and Sports':

When people discuss gender relations and sports, they usually focus on issues related to fairness and equity, as well as to ideology and culture, revolv[ing] around topics such as . . . gender inequities in participation, strategies for achieving equal opportunities for girls and women, the ways in which prevailing gender logic constrains lives . . . and subverts the achievement of gender equity, and the cultural changes required to achieve gender equity.[66]

Taken as a whole, these sport studies works typically reiterate female sportspersons as either subjugated by masculine hegemonies and

---

65. John Evans and Dawn Penny, 'Introduction: Setting the Agenda', in *Gender and Physical Education: Contemporary Issues and Future Directions*, edited by Dawn Penny (London: Routledge, 2002), 6–7. See also earlier important works that defined the subject area such as M Ann Hall, editor, 'The Gendering of Sport, Leisure and Physical Education', in *Women's Studies International Forum*, 10/4 (1987); Helen Lenskyj, *Out of Bounds: Women, Sport and Sexuality* (Toronto: Women's Press, 1986); Yvonne Zipter, *Diamonds are a Dyke's Best Friend* (Ithaca: Firebrand Press, 1988); GA Uhlir, 'Athletics and the University: The Post-Woman's Era', in *Academe*, 73/4 (1987), 25–29; Pat Griffin, *Strong Women, Deep Closets: Lesbians and Homophobia in Sports* (Champaign, IL: Human Kinetics, 1998). .

66. Jay Coakley, *Sport in Society: Issues & Controversies* (New York: McGraw Hill, 2007), 203. See also the same textbook, Ninth edition, 2007, 234–279 for updated discussion of the same issues. See also works such as John Harris, 'The Image Problem in Women's Football', in *Journal of Sport & Social Issues*, 29/2 (May 2005), 184–197; Barbara L Fredrickson and Kristen Harrison, 'Throwing Like a Girl: Self-Objectification Predicts Adolescent Girl's Motor Performance,' *Journal of Sport & Social Issues*, 29/1 (February 2005), 79–101.

discriminatory sexism; or, participation in athletics and sports is read in this research as a potentially liberating affair for both the human person and culture as a whole but only because freedom in this light is somehow in opposition to, or in conflict with biological nature.[67] A 2005 book published in the Routledge Cultural Studies/Sport Studies series decries:

> In a Western patriarchal context, the female body-subject is one that tends to be less sportively efficacious than its male counterpart. The space around the female is one that she has, through a process of socialization and enculturation, been discouraged from confidently reaching out towards.[68]

Studies explore the ways that modern women overcome physical and societal barriers to participate in sport. For example, the work of Amanda Roth and Susan Baslow, American ethics and political and feminist philosophers, on 'Femininity, Sports and Feminism: Developing a Theory of Physical Liberation':

> Although women and girls have been *doing* sports in great numbers . . . that participation has not . . .
> been . . . a liberating activity to the extent to which it can and should be . . . . We will show why sports have not resulted in a feminist liberation. We will then discuss what women would gain from physical liberation, why feminists have been hesitant to advocate it, and why they must overcome their concerns and do so.[69]

Most of these studies—as well as dominant popular culture—assume that sports participation is 'naturally' something that women desire to

---

67. See David L Schindler, 'The Significance of World and Culture for Moral Theology: *Veritatis Splendor* and the "Nuptial-Sacramental" Nature of the Body', in *Communio* 31 (Spring 2004), 118.

68. Hughson, Inglis and Free, *op cit*, 150.

69. Amanda Roth and Susan A Basow, 'Femininity, Sports and Feminism: Developing a Theory of Physical Liberation', in *Journal of Sport & Social Issues*, 28/3 (August 2004), 247.

do or that they should do; studies consequently criticise pop culture that depicts women in sport as a novelty or reversion. This line of research also includes studies in sport psychology/sociology that search for clues as to why girls drop out of sport; and research to understand what will motivate people to continue their exercise and sport involvement. Also prevalent in such literature is an ongoing suspicion of 'girlishness' or the 'feminine ideal' in sport. By this I mean female athletes are encouraged to beware or be critical of 'reproducing definitions of femininity,' 'constraining feminine bodies',[70] and to identify with masculine strength, power and athleticism.[71] For instance, I was recently a member of a dissertation committee in which the research sought to study the paradox of elite female athletes' gender performance—the author bemoaned that women athletes, even at intercollegiate, Olympic and professional levels, were culturally constrained to perform their gender in and outside of their athlete roles by applying make-up, wearing frilly clothes and doing their hair. As this dissertation did, some research argues that homophobia and threat of being identified as lesbian are powerful cultural factors that 'discourage many girls and women from playing sports or making sports an important part of their lives'.[72] Many current works about women in sport are critical of women's subordination in sport as reflected in how female athletes' bodies are a 'source of oppression' as they are 'forced' to 'appropriately' present themselves via 'body regimes' and acceptable forms of femininity, tagged 'the female apologetic'.[73]

In these renderings, women's freedom is diminished, for if they do participate in sports, they feel obligated to engage in such heterosexuality markings (appearing small, weak and quiet, wearing cosmetics, doing

---

70. Roth and Basow, 'Femininity, Sports and Feminism', in *op cit*, 249.
71. For example, the documentary *True-Hearted Vixens,* 2005, Berkeley Media DVD/VHS.
72. Griffin, *Strong Women, Deep Closets: Lesbians and Homophobia in Sport, op cit* as quoted in Coakley, *Sport in Society, op cit*, 211; Helen Lenskyj, 'Combating Homophobia in Sport and Physical Education', in *Sociology of Sport Journal*, 8 (1991), 61–69; Roth and Basow, 'Femininity, Sports and Feminism', in *op cit*, 253.
73. For example, Susan Birrell and Nancy Theberge 'Ideological Control of Women in Sport', in D. Margaret Costa and Sharon R.Guthrie, editors, *Women and Sport. Interdisciplinary Perspectives* (Champaign, IL: Human Kinetics, 1994), 341-360; Susan Bordo, *Unbearable Weight: Feminism, Western Culture and the Body* (Berkley: University of California Press, 1993).

hair, wearing ribbons, skirts, etc.). Also, in this and other research, the phenomenon of female athletes who fall prey to the beauty myth, questing through sports after a hard, heterosexualised body, whose 'function is to be gawked at by guys,' is understood as a problematic of societal 'gender logic'.[74] In this research there is a call to overcome 'the discourse of femininity,' to transform women's minds and bodies, theories and values.[75] I agree that gender logic, female apologetic, body regimes, etc *are* prevalent in sport—my essay does not refute the existence of these literary and anthropological understandings, but after such critiques, what are we to do? Again, I believe that elucidation might come from Christian theology.

There is no doubt that the work of scholars of women's sport who predominantly point out and seek to address practices and inherent inequities between men and women in sport has had a positive outcome. In the developed world of the past century, such research has contributed in striving towards social inclusion and equity in sport and commitments to laws that implement equity in physical education and sport curricula, activities, and organizations. There are efforts to work on dissolving stereotypical and prejudicial conceptions of femininity and masculinity and I applaud these responses. Among them are Susan K. Cahn's highly regarded *Coming on Strong: Gender and Sexuality in Twentieth-Century Women's Sport* that emphasizes the changing, nuanced definitions of femininity, making a call for 'attributes long defined as masculine—skill strength, speed, physical dominance, uninhibited use of space and motion—to become human qualities and not those of a

74. Andrea Solomon, 'Our Bodies, Ourselves: The Mainstream Embraces the Athlete Amazon. *The Village Voice* (April 2000), 19-25 accessed at www.villagevoice.com/issues/0016/solomon2.shtml 7 August 2004. See also Laura K Egendorf, *Is there Sexual Equality in Sports?* (San Diego: Greenhaven Press, 1999); 'Gendering Difference', in special issue of *Journal of Sport & Social Issues*, 27/1 (February 2003); David Hyland, 'When in Rome: Heterosexism, Homophobia and Sports Talk Radio', in *Journal of Sport & Social Issues*, 28/2 (May 2004), 136–168; Barbara L Fredrickson and Kristen Harrison, 'Throwing Like a Girl: Self-Objectification Predicts Adolescent Girls' Motor Performance,' *Journal of Sport & Social Issues*, 29/1 (February 2005), 79–101.
75. Roth and Basow, 'Femininity, Sports and Feminism', in *op cit,* 262.

particular gender'.[76] For example, Rachel Dilley builds upon Cahn's earlier work in her 2006 ethnographic study of female rock climbers:

> Zoë is an elite climber whose life is dedicated to climbing. She talked about the impact of the physical changes the male and female junior British team go through when they reach puberty, particularly in relation to the greater muscle strength developed by the boys, and the increase in the girls' body weight, without the same muscle gain. For me, this discussion with Zoë was a kind of a revelation because until then I had been thinking about men and women's climbing physicalities *only* in terms of a gendered discourse, which sets limits on women's abilities and bodies, and undermines women's achievements. I had forgotten about material bodies and the interconnections between material bodies and gendered discourse. An example of these interconnections can be seen in how routes and different styles of climbing are valued and judged . . . From the preliminary findings of my research I would suggest that within climbing alternative femininities are being lived.

Yet, even with scholars acknowledging these nuanced meanings of bodily attributes, As Dilley above does, I believe that for the most part, gender and sport studies lack serious dialogue with philosophies such as those put forth by John Paul II. Dilley for instance, concludes her study with a negative view of the 'binary at work' which positions 'women's climbing achievements as lesser than men's' when 'climbing femininities' are 'still being constructed as distinctly and innately different to climbing masculinities'.[77] The theology of the body dares us to imagine sport in

---

76. Susan K. Cahn, *Coming on Strong: Gender and Sexuality in Twentieth-Century Women's Sport* (Cambridge, MASS and London: Harvard University Press, 1994).

77. Rachel Dilley, 'Climbing Tales: Gendered Body Narratives and Stories of Strength,' Centre for Interdisciplinary Gender Studies, Conference Proceedings—'Thinking Gender—the NEXT Generation.' UK Postgraduate Conference in Gender Studies, 21–22 June 2006, University of Leeds, UK, e-paper no 14, 9, accessed at http://66.102.1.104/scholar?hl=en&lr=&q=cache:w9DZx9RY6KkJ:www.leeds.ac.uk/gender-studies/events/epapers/epaper14%2520Rachel%2520Dilley.pdf++%22rachel+dilley%22 on 16 January 2008.

a way that differences between male and female bodies/sport styles no longer matter in a modernist sense; from a General Audience talk at the Vatican, John Paul states, 'the body in its masculinity and femininity assumes the value of a sign—in a way, a sacramental sign [an ontological dimension with] ethical meaning'.[78]

Indeed, how does the thought of John Paul II challenge us about what it is to be a modern/post-modern person who plays, works, spectates, collects, administers and wonders about sport? First, he would agree with the emancipation of women and their right to equality in political and economic life. Yet, I believe that John Paul's philosophy can be read as a criticism of some aspects of modern feminism. For one, if gender is a social construction, John Paul sees this as liberating, not constraining. That feminine ideals have been overtaken by masculine ideals (in 1930 Christopher Dawkins explained, 'woman has been absorbed by the masculine order'[79]) would *not* be the root problematic of 'women in sport' as typically identified in sport sociology. In terms of sport culture, following John Paul II's thought, masculine sporting identities would not imply an opposite feminine subjectivity. That is, instead of focusing specifically on how women can develop their strengths and disrupt masculine cultural hegemony in sport cultures, 'femininity' in light of John Paul's ideas is not a falsity of personhood, but a gift of true self.[80] No matter one's state of (dis)ability, fitness or intellect, the person's existence is 'legitimate and charged with meaning'.[81] A simple example: Thus, the person in today's sports crazy world who is not interested in sport, does not speak sports' *lingua franca,* is *valued* instead of treated as

---

78. John Paul II, General Audience, October 22, 1980, 'The Value of the Body According to the Creator's Plan'. See also Karol Wojtyla, *The Jeweler's Shop* (London: Hutchison Publishing Group, 1980) (a play originally published in 1960 [but written much earlier] when John Paul was Bishop of Krakow) called 'a significant link' between the Pope's early thought on love, ethics, sexuality, etc.

79. Christopher Dawkin, 'The Background of Modern Feminism', review of Meyrick Booth, Woman and Society, October 1930, reprinted by permission of Julian Philip Scott at http://catholiceducation.org/articles/feminism/fe0032.html accessed on 19 December 2005.

80. For example, Schindler, 'Significance of World and Culture for Moral Theology,' *op cit,* 129-142.

81. Buttiglione, *Karol Wojtyla: The Thought of the Man Who Became Pope John Paul II, op cit,* 25.

a cultural oddity. As the current Pope Benedict XVI in earlier writings puts it, 'The being of the other is not absorbed or abolished, but rather, in giving itself, it becomes fully itself'.[82] Qualities such as strength, aggression, boldness and muscularity take feminine or masculine form, as Cahn above noted. Remember that the central notions emphasised by John Paul II's thought understand femininity and the culture of sport in light of Mary, Jesus' mother, as a model for humanity. Nowadays the human body is exalted as the purpose of human existence. Pope John Paul II's Mariology teaches that the human body becomes glorious by doing the will of God.

What would be the philosophy of such 'Marian' sport and what would such sport look like? Much of John Paul II's Mariology can be creatively applied to contemporary sport-related examples. For example, the topic 'sport/media' calls to mind many issues of magnitude associated with modernity including the subjects of privacy/voyeurism, role models, youth sport, fair labor, and environmentalism. John Paul's *Gospel of Life* addresses 'those involved in the mass media':

> need to present noble models of life and make room for instances of people's positive and sometimes heroic love for others. With great respect they should also present the positive values of sexuality and human love, and not insists on what defiles and cheapens human dignity. In their interpretation of things, they should refrain from emphasizing anything that suggests or fosters feelings of indifference, contempt or rejection in relation to life. With scrupulous concern . . . they are called to combine freedom of information with respect for every person and a profound sense of humanity.[83]

Jay Coakley's new *Sports in Society: Issues and Controversy* text, an excellent beginning (albeit still structured around achieving gender equity) lists possibilities including 'programs that embody an ethic of care

---

82. Joseph Cardinal Ratzinger, *The Spirit of the Liturgy* (San Francisco: Ignatius Press, translated by John Saward, 2000), 33.
83. John Paul II, 1995 Encyclical Letter *The Gospel of Life* (*Evangelium Vitae*), 98.

and connection between teammates and opponents'.[84] Coakley devotes
in-depth discussion to 'alternative definitions of femininity' suggesting
'gender equity will never be complete or permanent without changes
in how people think about masculinity and femininity and in how
sports are organised and played'.[85] Older work on the phenomenology
of bodily movement or 'humanistic pursuit for inquiry into the beauty
of sport'[86] may also be illustrative of a Christian vision of femininity and
sport. Yet, I want to make clear that when I discuss Marian sport, I do
not mean to imply 'girls'/women's sport,' 'sport for girls/women,' or
an exclusive female ontology/epistemology of sport. Marian sport is for
all of humanity.

Can I name some precise sports that may fulfill the Marian vision
outlined here? For a start, all sport showcases for us (as GK Chesterton
declared) 'the marvelousness of all things;'[87] how astonishing it is to
be human and alive through and from God. I suggest too, that Marian
sports may have the essence of sport as described by philosopher Gilles
Deleuze:

> Running, throwing a javelin and so on, effort, resistance,
> with a starting point, a lever. But nowadays, I see movement
> defined less and less in relation to a point of leverage. Many
> of the new sports—surfing, windsurfing, hang-gliding—
> take the form of entry into an existing wave. There's no
> longer an origin as starting point, but a sort of putting-
> into-orbit. The basic thing is how to get taken up in the
> movement of a big wave, a column of rising air, to 'come
> between' rather than to be the origin of an effort.[88]

84   Coakley, *op cit*, 276.
85   *Ibid*, 277.
86   Benjamin Lowe, *The Beauty of Sport: A Cross-Disciplinary Inquiry* (Englewood Cliffs NJ: Prentice-Hall, Inc., 1977), 269.
87   Gilbert Keith Chesterton and Alvaro De Silva, *Brave New Family: G.K. Chesterton on Men and Women, Children, Sex, Divorce, Marriage & the Family* (Ignatius Press, 1990), 183-184.
88. Gilles Deleuze, 'Mediators', in *Incorporations*, edited by Jonathan Crary and Sanford Kwinter (New York: Urzone, Inc, 1992), 281.

In this same vein, bodily performances such as Parkour, aesthetic performances such as *Circ de Soleil,* or troupes that blend sport, dance and musical composition— embodiments of Certeau's something *said-between* or Giorgio Agamben's *whatever*[89] may be close to Marian sport sensibilities:

> Project Bandaloop takes dance in a new direction by blending it with sport in the form of rock climbing and rappelling. Their latest project, *Crossings: Stories of Gravity and Transformation,* was originally performed during an 18-day crossing of the Sierra Nevada Mountains in California. Moving across the range from east to west, the company stopped to create site-specific work at beautiful places along the trail.[90]

Granted, such activities as listed above call for highly trained elite athlete-performers and/or have historically been undertaken by certain social classes of people,[91] or they might seem typically 'new age,'— yet this is not my intent, except to declare that the essence of these activities hints at corporeal realizations outside of the present culture of sport. Somehow, Marian sport activities perhaps are liminal[92] and exude excellence, the divine. Perhaps some will not be predominantly movement based, but virtual. Whatever their embodied or 'motile' form, sport can be imagined as supernatural, extraordinary, always implying a divine standard, knowledge of the good, with aesthetic and ethical components.

---

89. Giorgio Agamben, *The Coming Community: Theory Out of Bounds* (Minneapolis: University of Minnesota Press, 1993).

90. 'Project Bandaloop, Dance in a Different Light,' accessed on 11 January 2007 at <http://artsedge.kennedy-center.org/content/3496/>

91. For example, Catherine Palmer, '"Shit Happens"': The Selling of Risk in Extreme Sport,' *Australian Journal of Anthropology*, 13/3 (December 2002): 323-337.

92. Victor Turner, *The Forest of Symbols: Aspects of Ndembu Ritual* (Ithaca: Cornell University Press, 1967), 93–111; Arnold Van Gennep, *The Rites of Passage*, translated by B Vizedom and GL Caffee (Chicago: The University of Chicago Press, 1960, original 1909).

Indeed, to do away with modernist definitions of sport (such as earlier work by John Loy[93]) should be an aim of Marian sport studies. For example, today movements and aesthetics previously strictly defined as either 'dance' or 'sport' have been linked (in the United States, see the MTV's 'America's Best Dance Crew' as an example[94]). A positive aspect of the vibrant technological-consumerist renaissance of late may be the new ways that sport has grown beyond its Western 'canon' (sport 'canon' implies the descriptors 'young,' 'fit,' 'male,' 'team,' 'coach,' 'records,' 'rules,' 'uniforms,' 'spectators,' bureaucratization, pedagogies, etc.). Sport, art and music merge today on screens, in super slow-motion, holograms, in performances, on the streets. The emphasis in some advertising that is placed on the universal beauty of human movement, form, physical sacrifice, and bodily mortifications also has the capacity to be Marian - there is room for thinking more about mortification and asceticism practices associated with sport that inspire toward the good, as saints have long used them, but not as narcissistic or cultural practices that maintain the *status quo* (such as gymnasts who fast to meet coach or institutionalized sport expectations). The culture of sport in light of Mary may also universally lie already in the nooks of culture—the liminal spaces of play: dark yet at the same time spontaneous;[95] sport performativity that mortifies, renews a covenant with God. Certeau uses the gorgeous words, 'suffering dazzles' that we may perhaps connect to tentative visions of Marian inflicted sport:

> Suffering dazzles. It is already seeing, just as there are no visionaries but those stripped of self and of things by fascination with the misfortunes that occur. No, I speak of odd intimacies, there in the belly, here in the head, trembling, twitching, deformity, the rude brusqueness of a body unknown to others. Who would dare surrender them? Who would take them from us? They preserve us from strange retreats. They are our scraps of history, of

93. John Loy, 'The Nature of Sport: A Definitional Effort', in M Marie Hart, editor, *Sport in the Socio-Cultural Process* (Dubuque, Iowa: William C Brown, 1972).

94. http://www.mtv.com/overdrive/?id=1583319 accessed on 28 July 2008.

95. For example, Callois, *op cit*; Suits, *op cit*; Huizinga, *op cit*.

secret rites, of ruses, and of habits with shadows lurking in the hidden places of the body.[96]

Along with not being tied to strict definitions of sport, we might remember theories too, such as David Sansone, Benjamin Lowe, Johann Huizinga and Joseph Ratzinger,[97] about how sport is at its root an exceptional, erotic, universal, sacramental activity. I have pointed out the reluctance of scholars to engage with talk of Christianity-women-sport, but another taboo in cultural studies of sport circles, something missing from our projects of late, has been exploration of the idea that sport and all of its polyphonic, myriad peripherals[98] have a deeper social function in an 'organicist sense'.[99] I note 'of late', for thinkers such as CLR James saw sports not only as metaphors for society and politics, but also with a trans-historical function/value.[100] James argued for the importance

---

96. Certeau,'Suffering Dazzles', *op cit,* 156.

97. David Sansone, *Greek Athletics and the Genesis of Sport* (Berkeley: University of California Press, 1988); Paul Vernant, *Myth and Society in Ancient Greece,* translated by J Lloyd (New York: Zone Books, 1990), 260; Marcel Detienne and Paul Vernant, *The Cuisine of Sacrifice Among the Greeks,* translated by Paul Wissing (Chicago and London: The University of Chicago Press, 1989), 121; Thomas F Scanlon, *Eros and Greek Athletic* (Oxford and New York: Oxford University Press, 2002), 64-97; Lowe, *The Beauty of Sport: A Cross-Disciplinary Inquiry, op cit;* Callois, *op cit;* Joseph Cardinal Ratzinger, *The Spirit of the Liturgy, op cit;* Huizinga, *op cit.* See also René Girard, *Violence and the Sacred,* translated by Patrick Gregory (Baltimore: Johns Hopkins University Press, 1979); Richard Schechner, *The Future of Ritual: Writings on Culture and Performance* (London: Routledge, 1993); Schechner, *Performance Studies* (New York and London: Routledge, 2006), 1–6, 28–40, 49–57, 63–64, 89–122, 170-171, 244–248, 292–296.

98. By peripherals I mean anything, anyone and everything connected to sport in any way: mascots, trading cards, fans, coaches, manufacturers, sport history books, spectators' memories; museum artifacts, hot dog venders, pod-casts, souvenirs, tickets, playground rhymes, etc. See Robert Rinehart, *Players All: Performances in Contemporary Sport* (Bloomington: Indiana University Press, 1998).

99. On 'organicist' see Thomas F Scanlon, *Eros and Greek Athletics* (Oxford: Oxford University Press, 2002), 336, 366, 409.

100. James' perspective has been referred to as 'a gesture towards universalism that many argue is James' weak point.' See Benjamin Graves, 'Beyond a Boundary: The Aesthetics of Resistance,' *Political Discourse—Theories of Colonialism and Postcolonialism,* accessed on 20 April 2005 at http://www.thecore.nus.edu.sg/post/poldiscourse/james/james2.html

of sport in social history, using the ancient Greeks as beginning point, recognizing the holistic role that sport played within communities:

> We respond to physical action or vivid representation of it, dead or alive, because we are made that way. For unknown centuries . . . significant form in elemental physical action is native to us . . . they remain part of our human endowment.[101]

The 2007 monograph from film work by Roland Barthes, *What is Sport,*[102] based on the 1961 film *Le Sport et les hommes,* includes the correspondence of which Hubert Aquin, the director-producer of the film, had with Barthes. Aquin says 'What concerns us . . . is sport as a psychosocial phenomenon.' Barthes answers in the film and as published in the little monograph:

> What is sport? . . . . sport is a great modern spectacle cast in the ancestral forms of spectacle . . . At certain periods, in certain societies, the theater has had a major social function: It collected the entire city within a shared experience: the knowledge of its own passions. Today it is sport that in its way performs this function.[103]

This sport-as-spectacle has the capacity for beauty and Marian sensibility. Indeed, being a human person in the philosophy of John Paul II is about fulfilling longing for beauty, excellence, and truth by living in God's transforming power, as a part of Christ's body on earth (from Augustine, true happiness is joy born of the truth). This Marian femininity then, like radical femininity, is always in the act of being culturally constructed because of human free will. From Pope John Paul II's writings, we can begin a sports studies project with the premise that man and woman have unique masculine or feminine characters, endowed by God with a goodness and balance of humanity; earthly beings are forever on a journey of cultivating and exploring their male and female

101. CLR James, *Beyond A Boundary* (New York: Pantheon Books, 1963), 203–204.
102. Roland Barthes, *What is Sport?,* translated by Richard Howard, (New Haven and London: Yale University Press, 2007).
103. *Ibid,* 3, 45–47, 57, 59,

characters. Joined with John Paul II's thought, these ideas conceptualise solutions to issues associated with 'femininity and the culture of sport' as ultimately founded upon accounts of God as triune—reiterating the theme of the communion of bodies and self as gift. As man and woman continue to give themselves to each other, they affirm their masculinity and femininity while deepening awareness of it. They establish a bond that is at once reciprocal and communitarian. Graham Ward writes in *Cities of God:*

> Christian desire is always excessive, generous beyond what is asked. It is a desire not to consume the other, but to let the other be in the perfection they are called to grow into . . . It is a desire ultimately founded upon God as triune . . . A theological account of desire will describe alternative erotic communities, communities analogically related through desire . . . this theology starts from what it is to be called by God as an embodied soul to participate in Christ's body.[104]

John McClelland, in his article 'Eros and Sport: A Humanist's Perspective,' also applies this idea to sport:

> the erotic dimension of sport is not just in the 'bawdy pictures' found on Greek pottery or the animalistic desire to sexually possess an athlete with a perfect body. It is part and parcel of what raises us above the animals and makes us truly human: ruling ourselves, using language effectively, feeling strong emotions for another person, acquiring knowledge for its own sake, and improving our bodies by exercise and sport.[105]

In Christian theology, sin shattered this original integrity—this eros—of the person and the unity between male and female. In this fallen state, the body is no longer subordinated to the spirit and so its capacity to

104. Graham Ward, *Cities of God* (London and New York: Routledge, 2000), 77.
105. John McClelland 'Eros and Sport: A Humanist's Perspective', *Journal of Sport History,* 29/3 (Fall 2002), 405.

express the person is radically diminished; 'the unity between man and woman is replaced by suspicion and alienation'.[106] For John Paul II, discrimination against women in sport would echo Genesis 3:16, 'He shall rule over you,' words to the woman following original sin. In John Paul's theology of the body, domination and discrimination diminish the dignity of both sexes, but have more serious consequences for the woman who is made the object of male control (as sport feminists would for the most part agree).

Léonie Caldecott, who has written on the 'new feminism' of John Paul II, identifies 'the 'debt' owed by men to women, who pay the heaviest price for the bearing of life'[107] (again, this 'bearing of life' is not biological determinism, but a metaphor for the holding up of culture in a myriad of ways)—Caldecott identifies this idea of 'debt owed by men to women' (we aren't here on earth just for ourselves) as a key concept in the creation of John Paul II's new feminism that is liberating to culture. As I outlined above, in usual studies concerning femininity and sport, this paradigm of liberation, of openness, is prevalent. Why not put this idea in dialogue with John Paul II's conception of culture as forming 'a kind of organic whole with nature. It reveals the roots of our union with nature, but also of our superior encounter with the Creator in the eternal plan, a plan in which we participate by means of reason and wisdom'.[108]

In North American sport sociology, it is rare, or even taboo to deal with such alternative philosophy (as exemplified above by my brief review of selected literature), so I have tried in this essay to open a conversation about John Paul II's sometimes controversial themes. In light of the foundational thought on the theology of the body that I have overviewed, John Paul II's writings undergird a body of thought that promises to challenge our conceptualizations about femininity and sport and that at the least should be brought into our conversations about sport culture—these theology of the body teachings may lend to sport

---

106. John S Grabowski, 'Forward', *op cit*, 18.
107. Léonie Caldecott, 'Sincere Gift: The New Feminism of John Paul II', in Oddie, *John Paul the Great, op cit*, 122.
108. Karol Wojtyla, 'The Problem of the Constitution of Culture Through Human Praxis', in *Person and Community* (New York: Peter Lang, 1993), 269–270, as quoted by David L Schindler, 'Significance of World and Culture for Moral Theology: *Veritatis Splendor* and the 'Nuptial-Sacramental' Nature of the Body', in *op cit*, 127.

studies as well as popular sport activities an intellectual fullness and a radical phenomenology of bodily movement, play and contest.

There are many ways that my work here can be criticized but hopefully conversation and debate by others will ensue. Although my particular standpoint epistemology in this piece has been as a Christian-convert and sport/play studies scholar, I believe that regardless of one's standpoint, there is value in using Christian theology to approach the study of sport. There are distinct criticisms that can be made of my essay regarding areas that need fuller explanation: what is so unique about Christian theology? Is this a call for a return to the darkest ages of patriarchy? Are you caught up in false consciousness and pseudo-spirituality? What specifically of Lesbian-Gay-Bisexual-Transgendered athlete identities in Christian thought?

As I noted at the opening of this essay, I am not an expert in either Christian theology or gender studies, but I wanted at the least to suggest that Pope John Paul II's theology of the body interrupts the dominant mode of doing gender and sport studies because it declares: the body reveals God. Scholars like Judith Butler or Susan Bordo (whose works are often used as foundational to sport and gender studies) would have that this work restricts the meaning of masculinity and femininity.[109] However, just as in poststructuralist studies like Butler's, the theology of the body literature acknowledges the performative and socially constructed aspects of gender. Unique to the theology of the body, is that what a human does with his/her body makes a radical difference in the world because the body is understood as gift from God. Because feminine nature affords women distinct physical and spiritual capabilities with which to participate in the social order, modern dualism about women in sport is rejected in this theology of the body paradigm.

Over the past twenty years, it is common in cultural studies of sport and gender to exoticise particular sub-cultures and practices of women in sport. Yet I believe that this ethnographic work while very valuable, cannot continue to be relied upon to define the field of study. John Paul's theology of the body also offers a solution to a paradox that appears in many such sport studies: in many of the studies I critiqued above,

---

109. Judith Butler, *Gender Trouble: Feminism and the Subversion of Identity* (New York: Routledge, Kegan & Paul, 1990); Bordo, *Unbearable Weight: Feminism, Western Culture and the Body, op cit.*

women and men are assumed to be identical in given nature, yet in the same studies, women are depicted as naturally having from the start special caring ways, holistic spirituality, a special athletic sisterhood, etc. It is paradoxical on the part of secular studies of sport that on one hand, women athletes are supposed to have been socialized into gender roles governed by dominant hegemonies, but on the other hand, women in sport studies literature are at the same time depicted as possessing natural and unique capabilities, different from those of males. Jennifer Metz's work on motherhood, pregnancy and the Women's National Basketball Association is a case in point.[110] Metz weaves her longings to be wife/ mother into her scholarly ethnographic work about professional female basketball players. Reading between the lines, it is clear that Metz understands women as having special mothering characteristics, yet she ends up merely critiquing society's role in reproducing race and gender stereotypes. A bold approach to such auto-ethnographies may be to interject Christian beliefs, a concern for 'divine truth instead of worldly utility',[111] such as those articulated in John Paul's theology of the body. Beattie eloquently declares,

> A feminist sacramental vision needs to refocus its lens beyond liberal feminisms primary concerns of justice and equality in order to recognize that faith, hope and love provide a more textured language for the mystery of our humanity . . . I go in search of the strange hope of the Catholic faith in order to think redemption anew . . . I ask how feminist theology might rediscover the intimate and otherness of God of Christian revelation whom we encounter in the writings of mystics such as Catherine of Siena for whom God was a 'mad lover' who pursued her through all the struggles of her tormented spirituality and in Aquinas for whom creation was a wondrous window into the love of an utterly unknowable God . . . this invites

110. Jennifer L Metz, *Babes, Balls and Babies: A Working Ethnography of Motherhood* (unpublished doctoral dissertation, University of Illinois at Urbana-Champaign, 2005).
111. Woodhead, 'Spiritualising the Sacred', in *op cit*, 207.

a rediscovery of the language of mysticism and prayer as channels into new ways of knowing and being.[112]

I have tried to overview the promises of the theology of the body as that body of ideas can be applied to thinking about sport and femininity. To begin to do this, I critiqued works in sport sociology and secular critical-theory about the body and sport, and tried to show how Christian thought might seriously contribute to discernment concerning sport and femininity. Such a paradigm has promise for further developing ideologies about the calling that every human has—to belong to the universal church, to journey one's whole life to heaven, 'For you have been bought at a great price. Glorify God and bear him in your body'.[113]

---

112. Beattie, *New Catholic Feminism, op cit,* 7–9.
113. 1 Corinthians 6.20.

Chapter Five

Sport, Sailing And Human Spirituality

Richard Hutch

One could be reminded of humankind's first photographic glimpses of the earth from the moon taken by astronauts who arrived there in the late 1960s. For the first time in human imagination, such confirmation underscored that it was possible for people to envisage a role in the universe other than a central one. This was wondrous but also unnerving realisation, but not exactly a new insight into the relationship between humans and the cosmos. The astronomer, Copernicus, suggested a similar view of the cosmos during medieval times. His view eventually pushed aside the second century cosmology of Ptolemy, a Greek astronomer based in Egypt. However, until the time of Copernicus, Western civilisation developed along the lines of the Ptolemaic worldview, which the early Christian Church adopted. Ptolemy's vision placed the earth in the centre of a universe around which the sun revolved. Ptolemy and others believed that the cosmos itself was ruled over by the 'God of Abraham, Isaac and Jacob' and their subsequent sacred lineages, which included all Christian believers. The pivotal role in the history of this mythical scheme was assigned to Christ, who takes the place of wayward or 'sinful' humankind. Though he was killed, it was believed that Christ could not die. He was God's gracious gift to humankind, a sacrificial price that he was willing to pay for human redemption: Christ's crucifixion on the cross would lead to resurrection for all in the cosmic scheme of things. Such was the cultural system of the West for at least a millennium-and-a-half. Western culture was based on a story or myth that served to explain all of creation and human purpose within it.

And then along came Copernicus, a true critic of the Ptolemaic cosmos. Copernicus stood alone, risking his life and scholarly reputation in so far as he advocated an alternative picture of the cosmos. Using his telescope, a new invention of the time, he declared all of creation to be heliocentric, or sun-centred. Copernicus skilfully demonstrated that the earth revolved around the sun and, moreover, that the sun itself was actually not as central in the cosmos as his astronomical discoveries might at first suggest to the medieval mind: the sun was merely one of billions of suns in the universe. The sacred cosmos of Ptolemy's vision was not only challenged, but also began to fill the thinking of the *intelligentsia* thereafter (if not in the imaginings of the medieval peasantry) with a less sanguine story or myth, one that largely pushed aside humankind and the presumed trajectory of salvation through a Christ as Saviour. Notwithstanding the centuries-long cultural inertia and force of the cosmic vision of Ptolemy and the medieval ecclesiastical establishment, the so-called 'Copernican revolution' diminished the privileged stature granted to human beings by Ptolemy.

In our day, Copernicus' worldview was visibly confirmed by views of the cosmos from the moon during the 1960s and 1970s. All could now see that humankind, after all, was only marginal at best amidst the grand and dramatic forces of the universe. Following from this was the insight that no 'God' could be said to have a final say about what being human had come to mean. A thoroughly 'humanistic vision' was now imaginable, though it took centuries for the theological cosmos of the Middle Ages to be usurped in the public's imagination by such a new vision. Following from this, a new moral vision of being human: it was possible to imagine withdrawing from the hubris of centrality and to reframe new human self-understandings without recourse to Christianity. A person's identity was no longer a given (humans created in the 'image of God'), but a human construction with almost unlimited potential but for the limits imposed by mortality. Individuals now had to rethink the role of humankind in the cosmic scheme of things, doing so alone and without cultural constructs of the past (especially without theological ones). Nevertheless, by means of being far from the centre of things, humankind could now bear true witness to a new and wondrous cosmos and its place within it. This was a leap ahead in the consciousness stakes, one that continues to contribute to human evolution: to *bear witness* in such a way was to emphasise what it could possibly mean to be human, or to pause to reflect on the *morality of being human* as such: one could now ask, what *is* the value of *my* life? Can I *be* different? No one could ever be spared dying and death. Salvation was no longer the prerogative of God, but now it could well be thought to be in the hands of all too mortal individuals, if at all. The question which posed the greatest challenge and has perplexed human-kind ever since is, exactly what is the role of being human in the universe, given the new post-Copernican view of the cosmos?

The sea and lone yachtsmen upon it constitute an apt *microcosm* of the fluidity of the entire cosmos and the living earth within it. For single-handed sailors to bear witness to themselves and the sea (which is most morally poignant in times of helpless peril) is an act that can be filled with spiritual insight. As astronauts who have been into space affirm, the experience of bearing witness to earth from a cosmic vantage point beyond it usually carries with it a vague sense of spiritual insight which can have practical moral affects in their lives. Such experiences may not only prompt humility and evoke compassion for others, but they also may offer vitality and moral leadership to the world at large, even though shrunken in importance as the Copernican vision suggests. Taking to the sea in yachts, especially by oneself (with confidence or not), has similar potential. A sailor alone at sea is dwarfed and weakened by the vastness of the ocean and easily threatened by its fury.

*   *   *

Sport and spirituality are linked together in popular culture by the theme of personal challenge that may lead to enhanced living. In this sense, the topic of sport and spirituality frames in a microcosm the existential nature of human life in general, and the focus is on mortality. Brushes with death punctuate life in spite of progress and rationality, which otherwise typify modernity and our technological present. The theme of discerning elements of human existence 'beyond the realm of progress and rationality' that characterises modernity and has spawned high technology in our time is central to the intellectual focus of the history of religions.[1] The theme also is taken up in studies of how major accidents happen. Being inflexible and sticking to rigid plans often contribute much to accidents. After accidents, such plans become only empty 'memories of the future,' ones that had paradoxically deflected human attention from changing personal and environmental circumstances and

---

1.   Hans G Kippenberg, *Discovering Religious History in the Modern Age* (Princeton and London: Princeton University Press, 2002), xii.

thereby underscored one's peril.[2] According the existential philosopher of sport, Harold Slusher,

> When man faces death, he really faces life. Sport provides for a voluntary and regulated expression of this confrontation. Man tends to be most authentic when close to death. At this point there is no need to fake. The hunter must stop 'playing at being a hunter,' when he awaits the charge of a wild boar. Now the superficial and superfluous are not necessary. There is no one to impress. Now he faces the ultimate reality. Is man capable of passing the test? It is *real* ability that counts. It is rather paradoxical that man needs to escape the 'real' world (which might not be so *real* after all) and enter into the artificial realm of sport in order to determine the authentic self. He now must admit real existence of the self, something he usually can manage to avoid. To this degree, the man of sport is closer to truth. He learns his potentiality. He realises what, perhaps, he has already and always known—namely, who he is. He no longer needs or can fool himself . . . man is forced to realize his own worth.[3]

Often the impact of realising self-worth is projected on a cosmic scale. Religion commentator, Michael Novak writes,

> Sports are religious in the sense that they are organized institutions, disciplines, and liturgies; and also in the sense that they teach religious qualities of heart and soul. In particular, they recreate symbols of cosmic struggle, in which human survival and moral courage are not assured. To this extent, they are not mere games, diversions, pastimes. Their power to exhilarate or depress is far greater

---

2. Laurence Gonzales, *Deep Survival: Who Lives, Who Dies, and Why: True Stories of Miraculous Endurance and Sudden Death* (New York and London: WW Norton, 2003), 43–54.
3. Howard S Slusher, *Man, Sport and Existence: A Critical Analysis* (Lea & Febiger: Philadelphia, 1967), 206–207.

than that. To say "It was only a game" is the psyche's best defense [*sic*] against the cosmic symbolic meaning of sports events.[4]

This paper concentrates on one sport in particular to demonstrate this, namely, the sport of yacht racing and cruising. The focus is on the individual sporting person who takes to the sea in a sailing yacht, or the single-handed or 'solo' sailor. The basis of research for this study is a close reading of dozens of autobiographical accounts of such sailors, along with several interviews with solo circumnavigators of the globe. The aim is to determine if lessons for living are learned from such activity, ones that go to matters of lifestyle and larger than ordinary self-understandings. Recent scholarship on offshore sailing usually associates the sport with the utopian aspirations inherent in sailing subcultures and feelings of heightened aesthetic experience in the lives of individual sailors.[5] The paper's scope takes this association into account but also goes beyond it. It considers not only the sanguine aspects of offshore voyages, but also interruptions to utopian aspirations and heightened positive aesthetic experiences individuals may enjoy at sea. The argument of the paper is that such interruptions can give rise to new moral postures toward living. These postures represent invigorated spiritual meaning and purpose, a force for living that changes a person's overall outlook and daily lifestyle.

Such a focus carries forward the formative discussion in the psychology of religion about varieties of religious experience in the lives of individuals first raised in the Gifford Lectures of 1901–1902 on Natural Religion by William James, a foremost contributor to the history and phenomenology of religion. For James, religion is 'the feelings, acts, and

---

4.   Michael Novak, 'The Natural Religion.' *Sport Inside and Out: Readings in Literature and Philosophy*, edited by David L Vanderwerken and Spencer K Wertz (Fort Worth: Texas Christian University Press, 1985), 350–363; 353.

5.   See James Macbeth, 'Ocean Cruising'. *Optimal Experience: Psychological Studies of Flow in Consciousness*, edited by Mihaly Csikszentmihalyi and Isabella S. Csikzentmihalyi (New York: Cambridge Cruising: A Sailing Subculture', *Sociological Review*, 40 (1992): 319–334; and 'Utopian Tourists: Cruising is Not Just About Sailing', *Current Issues in Tourism*, 3 (2000), 20–34. Also see Mihalyi Csikszenmihalyi and Isabella S Ciskzenmihalyi, editors, *Optimal Experience: Psychological Studies of Flow in Consciousness* (Cambridge: Cambridge University Press, 1988), 214–231.

experiences of individual men in their solitude, so far as they apprehend themselves to stand in relation to whatever they may consider the divine'.[6] Religious experience comes in two general varieties for James. First, there is the gradual dawning of spiritual insight associated with manic elation ('sublimity'). James identified this type of lived experience as 'healthy-mindedness,' or a life lived without severe self-doubts. Second, there is foundation-shaking experience linked to ominous depression ('morbid compunction'). This type of lived experience James associated with the 'sick soul,' or a life lived always on the edge of profound self-doubt. What does James' typology of religious experience mean for a consideration of sport in life? How does it fit in with the emphases of Slusher and Novak on the crucial and passionate engagements with life that sport provides? Is sport a religious experience?[7]

On the one hand, 'healthy-mindedness' could be said to be like athletes achieving incremental improvement in sporting performances over time, where goals are set and training is designed to meet those goals. When those goals are being achieved athletes report a deep satisfaction with themselves. Often they refer to that feeling as 'being in the zone' or experiencing 'flow,' expressions which they associate with their top performances and goal-achievement.[8] On the other hand, what interested James most was the 'sick soul'. The person with this kind of

6.   William James, *The Varieties of Religious Experience: A Study in Human Nature* (London: Collier Macmillan, Ltd, 1961), 42.

7.   See WJ Morgan, 'An Existential Phenomenological Analysis of Sport as a Religious Experience', *Religion and Sport*, edited by Charles S Prebish (Westport, CT and London: Greenwood Press, 1993), 119–149.

8.   See Michael Murphy and Rhea A White, *In the Zone: Transcendent Experience in Sports* (New York: Penguin/Arkana, 1995); Andrew Cooper, *Playing in the Zone: Exploring the Spiritual Dimensions of Sports* (Boston: Shambhala, 1998); Michael Murphy, *The Achievement Zone: 8 Skills for Winning All the Time from the Playing Field to the Boardroom* (New York: Putnam, 1998); Mihalyi Csikszenmihalyi, *Creativity: Flow and the Psychology of Discovery and Invention* (New York: Harper Collins, 1996); *The Evolving Self* (New York: Harper Collins, 1993); *Finding Flow: The Psychology of Engagement with Everyday Life* (New York: Harper Collins, 1997); *Flow: The Psychology of Optimal Experience* (New York: Harper & Row, 1990); Mihalyi Csikszenmihalyi and Isabella S Ciskszenmihalyi, editors, *Optimal Experience: Psychological Studies of Flow in Consciousness* (Cambridge: Cambridge University Press, 1988); and Susan A Jackson and Mihalyi Ciskszentmihalyi, *Flow in Sports: The Keys to Optimal Experiences and Performances* (Champaign, Illinois: Human Kinetics, 1999).

lived experience goes beyond simple incremental athletic performance. Sanguine experiences of 'being in the zone' or in 'flow' rarely come to such individuals, who are instead usually wracked by personal torment. Nevertheless, experiences of torment go to the heart of the meaning of sport as an idiom of human morality and self-worth. This is captured well by what Michael Novak writes about spectators or sports fans:

> Fans are not mere spectators. If they wanted no more to pass the time, to find diversion, there are cheaper and less internally exhausting ways. Believers in sport do not go to sports to be entertained; to plays and dramas, maybe, but not to sports. Sports are far more serious than the dramatic arts, much closer to primal symbols, metaphors, and acts, much more ancient and more frightening. Sports are mysteries of youth and aging, perfect action and decay, fortune and misfortune, strategy and contingency. Sports are rituals concerning human survival on this planet; liturgical enactments of animal perfection and the struggles of the human spirit to prevail.[9]

Such a view of the meaning of sport represents the kind of engagement in life and self-doubt ('Will we win or lose?') that typifies individuals identified by James as 'sick souls', which he took to the be the most interesting kind of people to study and from whom to learn lessons about existence and the building up of human character.[10] How does this relate to yachting enthusiasts and, more specifically, to solo circumnavigating sailors themselves?

Life-threatening depression bears the greatest capacity to bring the global circumnavigation plans of single-handed sailors to a standstill in spite of high moments and aesthetic joys along the way. The sea forces a lone sailor to realise who he or she is. Defining sailing as a spiritual endeavour can be undertaken by analysing their reflections

---

9. Michael Novak, 'The Natural Religion', *Sport Inside and Out: Readings in Literature and Philosophy*, edited by David L Vanderwerken and Spencer K Wertz (Fort Worth: Texas Christian University Press, 1985), 350–363.
10. J Angelo Corlett, 'Virtue Lost: Courage in Sport', *Journal of the Philosophy of Sport*, 23 (1996), 45–57.

about sailing alone far offshore, and then probing those reflections for signs of a Jamesian spectrum of existential peril.* The argument put here turns on a distinction between what I call *technical self-reliance* and *moral presence,* with the latter ideally offering a counter-balance to the former. Technical self-reliance can be defined as being able to control one's circumstances at sea and to extend that control by means of relying on high-tech equipment installed in most modern yachts going around the world. A sailor relies on rational self-confidence and assumes this is enhanced by means of the use of cutting-edge technology even though breakdowns of self and equipment can occur at any time. An over-emphasis on technical self-reliance amounts to closing one's eyes to the possibility (and probability) of serious mishaps at sea. Moral presence is a counter-point to technical self-reliance. Moral presence can be defined as a practical and larger way to live life than is ordinarily the case. It is a lifestyle that is not self-serving, but paradoxically the opposite: a clear-sighted preparedness to accept necessary failure and defeat (as one must accede to the trajectory of human mortality and its simulacra during life), to eschew grandiose heroics when the chips are down and, nonetheless, to exercise courage with maximum practical and personal effect in the face of extreme and, mostly, adverse circumstances. Moral presence psychologically reframes technical self-reliance in a higher key, one that goes beyond hubristic and persistent assertions of a will to control events. Moral presence lessens the importance of technical self-reliance at sea. It does this by inserting human fallibility into a perhaps naïve dependence on technology and the assumptions about a person's capacity for rationality that undergird it.

This distinction can be illustrated from the recent local Australian sporting scene in the build-up to the 2004 Olympics in Athens. Technical self-reliance has recently been expressed by the practice of 'doping' by athletes. The issue of 'doping' in competitive athletic performances is an application of high technology to the human body (a pharmacological extension of human capacity). The issue of the use of performance-enhancing drugs in sport is contentious not only because it makes for uneven competitions, but also because it shifts consideration away from sport as an existential test that could well bring about failure, albeit with increased human meaning about one's life-commitments. Moral presence was recently illustrated by the twenty-one year old Australian swimming wonder, Ian Thorpe, who is considered by many as Australia's most accomplished swimmer to date. During trials in the 400-metre freestyle heats for the 2004 Olympic Games, Thorpe accidentally lost his balance and fell off the blocks of the pool before the starting bell sounded. There was absolutely nothing he could do about it once his balance was lost and he began to tumble into the pool. He was automatically disqualified from competing in that event and, hence, from the possibility of going to the Olympics in Athens to represent Australia in the 400-metre freestyle event. The swimmer and the public united in anguish as they realised what had happened. It was not supposed to be that way, but the reality of the loss of control and being helpless to do anything to recover from it made a sporting event into high human drama. People urged Thorpe to lodge a protest, but he went silent about it, preferring to abide by the judges' decision. The event stopped a nation, even evoking emotional comment from the then Australian Prime Minister, John Howard. One journalist quoted Thorpe:

> 'Although it doesn't seem fair, and in a lot of cases life isn't fair, you just have to deal with it . . . I'm not so unlucky or unfortunate'. As the journalist went on to report, 'Thorpe show(ed) all those who seek the limelight, in any field, what leadership and character are all about . . . Thorpe has set the benchmark for grace in adversity. He has moved from being a great sportsman with nice manners into a genuine leader. For someone who has experienced only success, that capacity to deal with disappointment will prove more important than one more gold medal . . . For a country that has become seriously wealthy over recent decades but has seen the decline in many of the institutions that provide it a moral compass, it is important to have Thorpe and his colleagues in the public eye . . . Thorpe has shown much older men that real leadership is rising above your instincts.'[11]

---

11. Gregory Hywood, *Sydney Morning Herald*, 1 April 2004, 15.

The Thorpe event and the existential complicity of the public in it well illustrate the difference and interplay between moral presence and technical self-reliance.

Such an illustration can be distilled into something more abstract and applicable across a range of sporting activity in which the focus is on the lone individual. According to Harold Slusher,

> Facing death makes the man of sport available to an awareness of authentic existence. Perfor-mance, faced with such extreme stakes, will tend to represent authentic being. Putting it another way, man is rarely as moral as when he is facing death. Death tells man to 'face up' to life. Meaning comes to the performer when he becomes aware of the end. The totality is taken into account.[12]

Yachting people rely heavily on high technology in their sport, less so on simply 'being human'.[13] A case is put for 'being human,' or what can be understood as being morally present in yachting, at least more so than is currently done by sporting people in general and the yachting fraternity in particular. Being morally present is a values-stance in living, an orientation of the self where respect for human limitations assumes an increased importance in living. Such respect moderates the prospects that would otherwise appear to be limitless. Being morally present is an antidote to personal *hubris* and also to the human desire to control all of life's events. Moral presence flows from passionate participation in living in terms of what counts most. It can make for a meaningful life through sport, including yachting. Moral presence creates for many sporting individuals a 'genuine option' for living according to William James.[14] Being morally present is synonymous with spirituality; getting there constitutes human 'spiritual formation' without any philosophical or theological trappings.

---

12. Slusher, *op cit*, 207.
13. John M Hoberman, 'Sport and the Technological Image of Man', *Philosophic Inquiry in Sport*, edited by William J Morgan and Klaus V Meier (Champaign, Illinois: Human Kinetics, 1995), 202–208.
14. James, *op cit*, 32–62.

There are two experiential dimensions of moral presence. Both indicate how to 'face up to life', or how to cultivate what Slusher calls 'authentic existence' and James calls passionate participation in a 'genuine option' for living, rather than carrying on ignoring such personal tests. According to Laurence Gonzales, a well-known researcher in the field of survival in extreme environments, the two dimensions can be characterised by aphorisms. The first is 'Be here now,' or the experience of Zen mind.[15] This means that chances of survival increase if one can transcend past plans and future prospects, and then focus on the present. Accompanying this among those who survive in extreme circumstances is the realisation that they are overcome with wonder and marvel about small details of the environment into which they have been thrown. For example, a mountain climber who broke his leg could no longer be supported by his climbing partner, who held him by a rope from higher up the snow-covered mountain face. The partner was forced to cut the rope in order to save himself. The climber who was dangling from the end of the rope then fell into a crevasse of snow and landed on a narrow edge of ice on the side of a dark cavernous chamber inside the mountain. After an almost miraculous feat of survival crawling foot by foot out of the chamber and down to his base camp thousands of metres below, he reported not thinking about his dire circumstances but about how beautiful the inside of frosty chamber appeared glinting in the sunlight that penetrated from the slit above.[16]

The second experiential dimension of moral presence is 'Everything takes eight times as long as it's supposed to', or survival seems to take forever.[17] By focusing on the present, breaking down large crises into small, more manageable tasks is invited. This involves a 'one step at a time' approach rather than trying to overcome perilous circumstances by investing increasing amounts of effort to correct them. Accepting friction as a fact of life rather than trying to overcome it is the key. The harder a person tries to overcome life's friction, the more complex becomes his or her plan for reducing friction, and the worse things get. As Gonzales puts it, ' . . . plan for everything to take eight times as long

---

15. Gonzales, *op cit*, 121.

16. See the epic story in full in Joe Simpson, *Touching the Void: The Harrowing First-Person Account of One Man's Miraculous Survival* (New York: HarperCollins, 1988).

17. Gonzales, *op cit*, 121–122.

as you expect it to take. That allows for adaptation to real conditions and
survival at the boundaries of life and death, where we seek our thrills'.[18]
Consciously setting goals and then achieving them over the long haul is
what counts in crises. Sailors alone at sea are familiar with reducing sail
area ('reefing') in gales, which takes a step-by-step procedure that can
last for several hours during which being swept off a yacht is perilously
possible in spite of being harnessed to a hard point on deck. Panic can
lead to trying to reduce sail in one fell swoop in such circumstances, and
this could increase such moments of danger beyond control.

Moral presence can be cultivated best when a hitherto perhaps happy
reliance on technology at sea breaks down and little else can be done
in the face of serious peril.[19] A sailor is forced to 'face up' to life. Here
a sporting performance ends and the making of self-worth begins. The
responses of sailors to such issues vary, of course, but those who move
beyond considerations of technical aspects of yachting begin to reckon
in their own ways and in their specific contexts, or 'sailing spaces'
potent with meaning, with the morality of being as a source of human
happiness. According to one researcher, there are two strategies to
realising happiness in life.[20] The first, typically Western, is 'optimising' in
which the optimiser seeks to subdue the world, or make it conform to his
or her desires. The second strategy is characteristic of Eastern approaches
to happiness, or 'adapting'. Adaptors change and conform their desires
to the world. While the adaptive approach is attractive to those who
wish to make their happiness invulnerable, the optimising approach
to invulnerability depends on power and control over the world that
humans just do not possess. Hence, hubris is a ready potentiality for
optimisers in a way it is not for adaptors. The risk of simply adapting
to circumstances is a possible impoverishment of life, but this must be
balanced with reasonable optimising if life is to be enhanced. Sailors
who come to a realisation that being an adaptor is a better option than
being an optimiser undergo an internal shift of value-in-action, namely,
from *doing things* to survive at sea to *being who they truly are*, stripped of

18.   *Ibid*, 122.
19.   Jeffrey P Fry, 'Sports and 'The Fragility of Goodness', *Journal of the Philosophy of Sport*, 31 (2004), 34–46.
20.   Steven Luper, *Invulnerability: On Securing Happiness* (Chicago and La Salle, Illinois: Open Court, 1996), 6, 17, 45–46.

most illusions as they face the mirror of the impartial sea. They see in that mirror their own helpless, chaotic turmoil that human will cannot calm. Moral presence becomes a viable human stance in the face of peril at sea when other more technical options no longer suffice. Life-changing idioms of moral presence may often take hold. They are ways in which self-worth as a human being is discovered during yachting alone, as well as realised in a wide range of sports that focus on sporting performance by individuals and what happens when achieving desired performance goals fails (for example failure to repeat one's personal best time, or 'PB').

I shall note three idioms of moral presence under sail, which together are a phenomenology of single-handed sailors' lived experience at sea. However, a worst-case scenario is instructive first. What happens when complete faith is put in technical self-reliance at all costs (an 'Indestructible Titanic Complex,' perhaps), or when hubris tragically pushes moral presence entirely beyond a sailor's reach? Can happiness be achieved in such a way, or is such a strategy patently counter-productive? How can life at sea be optimised while at the same time adapt to the ever-present dangers faced by single-handed sailors?

Technical hubris at sea

Engineer Donald Crowhurst had tragic recourse to a delusion that he was an emissary from the farthest reaches of the universe with esoteric truths to impress upon humankind. He became a man under sail alone at sea whose plans to show the world his genius and skill turned quickly into only 'memories of the future'.[21] This future became an abysmal fate in so far as he failed tragically to account for his changing personal and environmental circumstances. Nothing granted Crowhurst a 'reality check', so to speak. He soared in a world of grandiosity all his own. This played itself out technically by means of his unusual inventions never before countenanced by the yachting fraternity (perhaps rightly so). His electronic gadgetry and "self-righting" device on his trimaran, which were purported to be revolutionary developments, never worked. His *pièce de resistance* for technical innovation on trimarans was his system for preventing total capsizes. If the boat heeled or tilted past the 'flipping

---

21. See Gonzales, *op cit*, 18.

zone' of fifteen degrees or more, electrodes in the side of the hull would signal a switching device that Crowhurst called his 'computer'. Peter Nichols, who chronicles Crowhurst's participation in the first 'solo' around the world yacht race during the late 1960s, describes the way in which the device was envisioned to work:

> [the] switching mechanism . . . would fire off a carbon dioxide cylinder connected to a pipe inside the hollow mast, which would inflate a buoyancy bag at the top of the mast. This would prevent the boat from completely capsizing. At that point, partially inverted, Crowhurst would pump water into the upper hull, which, as it grew heavier, would push downward and eventually flip the trimaran back upright.[22]

Such a feature sounds like a good idea, but when builders sat down and actually tried to make such a device they were faced with almost insurmountable difficulties. The inflatable bag would have to be so large *vis-à-vis* the trimaran that its weight would destabilise the vessel from above. This would require a lower mast to counteract the problem of top-heaviness. Crowhurst told the builder of his yacht that he had issued publicity everywhere indicating that the features of the self-righting device 'had been tested and were "now operating successfully" and were the results of a "development project" by Electron Utilisation Ltd', his then faltering engineering company.[23]

No such 'development project' ever took place. Moreover, Crowhurst's onboard 'computer,' as he called it, was projected to 'electronically monitor stresses in the rigging, sounding warning lights and alarms if loads became critical. Hooked up to a wind-speed indicator,' says Nichols, 'it would automatically ease sheets and sails'.[24] All of this, and other preparations for safety at sea, were total failures. How did Crowhurst react? Technical failures led to extraordinary means to regain control of his perilous situation alone at sea. Crowhurst fudged his logbook, in fact keeping two separate logbooks. One was his actual

---

22.   Peter Nichols, *A Voyage for Madmen* (Sydney: HarperCollins*Publishers*, 2001), 90.
23.   *Ibid*, 90. Crowhurst is quoted by Nichols.
24.   *Ibid*.

log of merely bobbing around in the South Atlantic Ocean for 243 days and 16,591 nautical miles between England and Uruguay during the 1968–1969 Golden Globe Race from England and back, all this while the other contenders sailed around the world alone, non-stop and unassisted as they were supposed to do. The other logbook was falsified to depict a global circumnavigation. The former represented Crowhurst's mood swings between mania and depression, while the latter sketched out how he ideally wished to understand himself even though deep in his heart-of-hearts he knew otherwise.

When he rejoined the fleet sailing back to England Crowhurst managed to manoeuvre his yacht, *Tiegnmouth Electron*, into second position just north of the Equator on his way to England. He was satisfied to be second because this would mean that race officials would not inspect his log-book(s). Only the logbook of the winner of the Golden Globe would be inspected for accuracy, seeking congruence between the record contained in the daily logbook and any corroborating evidence like radio reports of positions and sightings during the global voyage. However, fate took an ironic and cruel turn for Donald Crowhurst. The front-runner's yacht got holed by floating debris and pulled out of the race; Crowhurst was catapulted into the leading position by default. When he heard about this on his radio and subsequently realised that his fraud would be discovered, he made a fateful decision. A reconstruction of the scene after his empty yacht and its logbooks were found floating in mid-Atlantic points to the high probability that he perished at sea by his own hand, slipping quietly over the side amidst his psychotic turmoil and confabulation of self-importance.

Crowhurst's final entries describe his unshakeable conviction that he could leave his body and make himself divine whenever he wanted to. He underwent delusional ego-inflation without bounds. Alas, he argued the case for his belief on the basis of the mathematical puzzle, namely, the square root of minus one, which he believed was a powerful mystery. Just as the square root of minus one can turn ordinary numbers into 'imaginary' ones, which would be inconceivable to stalled minds, his new idea could turn ordinary thinking into unimagined forms:

> I introduce this idea [the square root of minus one] because [it] leads directly to the dark tunnel of the space-

time continuum, and once technology emerges from this tunnel the 'world' will 'end' (I believe about the year 2,000, as often prophesied) in the sense that we will have access to the means of 'extra physical' existence, making the need for physical existence superfluous. In the process the 'mechanism of second sight' and 'prophecy' will be laid bare as a process simply linked with the possession of intelligence, and likely to be possessed by all intelligent animals. It is the application of intelligence that will allow this mechanism to be used at will as a *superfluous by-product*.[25]

Such a delusional worldview buffered his imminent fraud. Like the ancient gazer Narcissus, he refused to see the deeper truth of his state of being amidst his circumstances at sea. These were masked by his tragic delusions of control in the face of failure. He assumed himself to be no ordinary mortal, but one for who sound seamanship was now trivial in his cosmic scheme of things. Attempts to manage unrestrained hubris and the possibility of humiliation that is often implied in the process is an agonising human experience.[26] Crowhurst unconsciously resolved at the end of the Golden Globe that moral presence of any degree was beyond his grasp.

Phenomenology of moral presence at sea

Moral presence is an existential counterpoint to the breakdown of technical self-reliance at sea, or failures of sporting performance. It appears in sailors' lives in three characteristic ways, and becomes evident in their autobiographical reflections on risk-management and self-worth at sea. The three ways are,

---

25.   Nicholas Tomalin and Ron Hall, *The Strange Voyage of Donald Crowhurst* (Camden, Maine: International Marine, 1995), 239. (Crowhurst's logbook is quoted.)

26.   See Mike McNamee, 'Hubris, Humility and Humiliation: Vice and Virtue in Sporting Communities', *Journal of the Philosophy of Sport*, 29 (2002); William I Miller, *Humiliation: And other Essays on Honor Social Discomfort and Violence* (London: Cornell University Press, 1993); and N Fischer, 'Competitive Sport's Imitation of War: Imagining the Completeness of Virtue,' in *Journal of the Philosophy of Sport*, 29 (2002).

- Techincal Finesse
- Cosmic Quest
- Personal Test

Each will be elaborated by way of illustrations from a number of sailors' lives at sea and their thoughts about their nautical experiences.[+]

First, moral presence may appear as the *technical finesse* of Robin Knox-Johnston, who skilfully avoided possible excesses of technical hubris and won the Golden Globe of 1968–1969. For him, the kind of spirituality that he found at sea always gave rise to pragmatic outcomes, or a 'God helps those who help themselves' point of view. As he put it after rounding Cape Horn and taking stock of the readiness of his yacht, *Suhaili*, to make the final run up the Atlantic to the finish line in England,

> The sea and ships are great levellers. There is certainly no room on a small boat for a person who is incompetent or won't pull his own weight . . . All share the same risks in a storm, and no earthly influence will select you above the rest to be saved if the ship founders . . . Their whole existence depended on their ability to come to terms with the wind and sea, and to use these forces to drive their ship . . . It is not surprising that most [seamen] thought more of their counterparts ashore about the cause of these forces, and not in the least surprising to me that so many were superstitious or developed unshakeable religious beliefs, and sometimes both. I have found myself thinking deeply on the matter when out in rough weather on a small boat. It is all very well for someone sitting in an office to explain logically how the waves can build up before the wind, for we have discovered the natural laws that control this, but to a seaman, the explanation of these laws does not always seem sufficient . . . the rules are there, the physical laws that we have slowly learned. If we obey them we have a chance of survival.[27]

---

27. Robin Knox-Johnston, *A World of My Own: The Single-Handed, Non-Stop Circumnavigation of the World in Suhaili* (New York: Morrow, 1969 & 1970), 172–173.

There is 'action through non-action,' which is the Chinese Taoist doctrine of *wu-wei*.[28] An example of *wu-wei* is the natural wearing down of rough stones into smooth pebbles over time in a flowing stream. Human gestation is similar, requiring little effort other than the virtual passivity induced by pregnancy. Moral presence is a similar inner or 'spiritual' posture assumed by sailors as they learn to get used to the sea. If they are lucky, then they come to learn that there is much that can be accomplished by taking action balanced by 'non-action' after all. Writes Knox-Johnston,

> It is no use knowing that your boat is heading towards the eye of a storm and praying to God to see you through it safely. That's not his job. It's your task to steer the boat away from the eye, and you are asking too much if you expect the boat to survive when you deliberately ignore the rules. My own philosophy is developed about the phrase, "The Lord helps those who help themselves." It is no good lying in your bunk, listening to the rising wind and feeling the boat beginning to strain and praying for God to take in reef. No one but a fool would expect anything to happen. One has to get up and reef the sails oneself before the boat's movement will ease . . . When everything has been done that you know you can do, you put your trust in your Superior Being, and just hope that what you have done is right . . . Because of this belief, throughout the voyage I never really felt I was completely alone, and I think a man would have to be inhumanly confident and self-reliant if he were to make this sort of voyage without a faith in God.[29]

A statement like this one testifies to Knox-Johnston's sense of achieved Zen-like 'wisdom,' which is perhaps as the psychoanalytic

28. See in general Arthur Waley, *The Way and Its Power: A Study of the Tao te Ching and Its Place in Chinese Thought* (New York: Grove Press, 1958); and *Confucius, Confucian Analects: The Great Learning; The Doctrine of the Mean*. Translated, with critical and exegetical notes, prolegomenon, copious indexes, and dictionary of all characters by James Legge (New York: Dover, 1971).
29. Knox-Johnston, *op cit*, 172–173.

thinker, Erik Erikson, puts it, namely, a capacity for 'detached concern for life itself in the face of death itself,' albeit with occasional recourse to religious thoughts and behaviours.[30] The achievement of such wisdom is a spiritual endeavour.

Second, moral presence may invoke a large and purposeful *cosmic quest* as it did for Bernard Moitessier, who felt driven to circumnavigate the globe as long as his food, water and stamina allowed, opting out of the Golden Globe of 1968–1969 entirely. If it can be said that Knox-Johnston carried forward a mainly competitive style of yachting as racing, then Moitessier represents a more leisurely style of yachting as cruising. For Moitessier, spirituality meant drawing close to the elemental sea and believing it to be infused with a life-giving mystical force, a power that could be made one's own. For example, there is no better illustration of his resistance to keeping and using high technology on board his yacht, *Joshua*, as his means of communicating his progress during the race.

The staff of the *Sunday Times* were eager to get as much publicity for their newspaper as possible by featuring frequent stories about Moitessier's voyage. They offered the Frenchman equipment that he had never before owned. The skipper of *Joshua* came to resent such offers, but mellowed towards key staff once they took into account his views about just how much equipment was needed. Writes Moitessier,

> . . . I stopped resenting the staff of the Sunday Times . . .
> Robert, the head of the team, would have liked me to ship
> a big transmitter with batteries and generator. They offered
> it gratis . . . so [I] could send them two weekly messages.
> The big cumbersome contraptions were not welcome. [My]
> peace of mind, and thereby [my] safety was more important,
> so [I] preferred not to accept them . . . Steve, . . . from the
> Press Service, loaded [me] with film, as well as watertight
> Nikonos cameras . . .'[31]

---

30. Erik Erikson, *Insight and Responsibility: Lectures on the Ethical Implications of Psychoanalytic Insight* (New York: WW Norton, 1964), 109–157 ('Human Strength and the Cycle of Generations'), 133.

31. Bernard Moitessier, *The Long Way*, translated by William Rodamur (London: Adlard Coles, Ltd, 1973; originally published Paris: Arthaud, 1971), 5.

While a transmitter and batteries is one thing, a fancy camera was a manageable concession. The problem arose with timing: how would pictures be able to be sent to the newspaper in lieu of radio broadcasts in order for the Press Service to report on the race day by day, week by week? Moitessier reached back into the arsenal of his youth in Hanoi for a solution, namely, his tried and true and trusty slingshot and a packet of fresh properly sized wide rubber bands:

> I preferred my old, quiet friend the slingshot to two or three hundred pounds of noisy radio equipment, but [Steve] could feel the 'how' and 'why' and helped me to find good rubber bands, supplying me with aluminium cans to contain messages I would shoot onto passing ships. A good slingshot is worth all the transmitters in the world! And it is so much better to shift for yourself, with the two hands God gave you and a pair of elastic bands. I will try to send them messages and film for their rag. It would make them so happy . . . and me too.[32]

One reads with delight how perplexed and amazed sailors on passing ships were to see Moitessier on his yacht shooting his message and film-filled cans into the air in the direction of their ships, which then accurately fell on board in one shot and clinked across the deck to be retrieved by crew. News of *Joshua* would then be wired back to London by the captains, and the photographs would be passed on to the nearest British Consul and posted to the *Sunday Times* by diplomatic courier. Moitessier's slingshot was technically efficient but primitive or, perhaps better, simple. Moitessier did not care. Moderating any urge to get carried away by modern marine technology was the priority of sustaining a mystical sense of purpose and relationship with the natural elements.

The matter of a camera and film took his memory back several years when he sailed from Tahiti to Alicante, Spain with his wife, Françoise: '. . . we never dared take pictures of the sea before the Horn, and least of all our big gale in the Pacific. Not because of danger or fatigue, but

---

32. *Ibid*, 5–6.

because we felt, in a confused sort of way, that it would have been a kind of desecration.'[33] He was convinced that destiny controlled the moral nature of men and women as did the stars of the horoscope, but also that destiny allows a person a range of technical options with which to play out one's moral nature in history, from event to event: 'Destiny deals the cards, but we play them'.[34] He often waxed lyrical about his solitude and likened himself to a seagull:

> I felt such a need to rediscover the wind and the high sea, nothing else counted at that moment . . . All *Joshua* and I wanted was to be left alone with ourselves . . . You do not ask a tame seagull why it needs to disappear from time to time toward the open ocean. It goes, that's all, and it is as simple as a ray of sunshine, as normal as the blue of the sky.[35]

Moitessier sees himself as a sea mystic in tune with the elemental forces that bathe in natural wonder.

Third, moral presence may also come in the form of a *personal test* for sailors who are realistically unsure of their skills, but who also are bold enough to embark on an offshore voyage alone in order to do their very best in the face of such a challenge. Australian Kay Cottee lacked self-confidence at the outset, but recouped heaps of it during her record circumnavigation of 1988 (first woman in record time, 189 days). Nearing Cape Horn is a major emotional, technical and symbolical event in the life of any solo yachtsman, more so than approaching and rounding any of the other four capes along the way. Cottee's autobiography comes to something of a crescendo of feeling that is mostly sublime in an aesthetical sense, but also physically demanding. The description of the beauty of the heaving Southern Ocean is perhaps one of the most captivating portrayals of the sea at its elemental best and worst, a powerful personal epiphany or primordial experience of *mysterium tremendum et fascinans*.[36]

---

33. *Ibid*, 26–27.
34. *Ibid*, 33.
35. *Ibid*, 3.
36. See Rudolf Otto, *The Idea of the Holy*, translated by John W Harvey (New York: Oxford University Press, 1958; first published 1917).

The *mysterium tremendum et fascinans* is not an ordinary lived experience, but an extraordinary event in the life of an individual, one that does not immediately make sense as it is beyond rationality and too powerful to contain. The *mysterium* means 'mystery' in the sense of the unknown and unknowable; it is the 'sacred'. *Tremendum* is that face of the sacred that induces feelings of awe and fear when an extraordinary event is experienced, and it always combines with the face of *fascinans*, feelings of fascination, allure and a sense of the sublime. Like a moth before a flame, a person who undergoes and experience of *mysterium tremendum et fascinans* must reckon with a coincidence of opposites, ones that could well conspire to create and destroy the self all at the same time. Just 585 miles from Cape Horn and in winds of fifty-five knots, Cottee comes as close as she ever gets to undergo a personal epiphany:

> It wasn't easy trying to slow down the boat. The further south we went the higher were the seas, as in the south latitudes of the Southern Ocean there is no land mass to break the speed and size of the waves as they hurtle round the globe. By 1600 hours we were under bare poles, towing the sea anchor, still doing a steady 7-plus knots and surfing up to 12 knots on the breakers. I tried setting the storm jib again and backing it with the helm down to put the boat into irons. After all my efforts I remember standing below, looking out of the clear companionway slide and watching the sea anchor, towed behind on the end of 10 metres of chain plus 70 metres of line, bouncing down the face of the next wave after the one we were riding. I estimated the waves to be approximately 20 metres high and breaking with a nice curl. When we were in the troughs I looked up, and despite my fears of being pitchpoled I was captured by the beauty of the aquamarine colours of the sun shining through the peak of the next approaching wave.[37]

Such an epiphanous moment became physically incarnate, the *mysterium* presenting its perhaps more destructive *tremendum* face.

---

37. Kay Cottee, *Kay Cottee, First Lady: A History-Making Voyage Around the World* (South Melbourne: Macmillan, 1989), 192.

Cottee's physical tension at the time was unshakable. With the Horn approaching, she writes,

> The tension was really getting to me. My shoulders felt stiff and my neck hurt badly since I had put it out a few days ago winching the storm jib up. There were tingles down my spine and my hands continually went numb. I was increasingly worried that I couldn't relax enough to get my neck to click back into place. If I settled into that position, permanent damage could be done. But no show of relaxing tonight, with land only a few miles away.[38]

Blackmores First Lady was rounding Cape Horn in mid-January 1988. Cottee's protracted personal epiphany progressed from a sense of destructive power that could not be controlled, even when it became embodied in the contorted vertebrae of her neck, to a fresh sense of excitement and personal accomplishment:

> After all the stories I had read about this ocean graveyard, here we were, only a few miles from it. I had thought it would give me a spooky feeling, considering the number of sailors who had been dashed to death on the treacherous black cliffs, or drowned in the mountainous seas. But my prime emotion was excitement and I had a great sense of accomplishment that I had reached what I then perceived to be the major obstacle in the voyage.[39]

Hiding deep within herself was a fear of rounding Cape Horn, but she now was doing it in the light of day and fully conscious of how far beyond that inner fear she was then growing. As a fitting ritual gesture to commemorate the powerful event that had come good, Cottee opened the Cape Horn present that had been given to her by her mother, a bottle of her favourite 'Joy' perfume. 'I sprayed myself with the lovely scent, then put on some lipstick, before sitting down to a delicious belated

---

38. *Ibid*, 74.
39. *Ibid*, 77.

lunch of fresh bread with crab and mayonnaise and the remainder of the bottle of Grange'.[40]

Cottee used the sea and the fine balance between action and non-action to test herself not only as a self-reliant technical sailor, but also as a moral being in formation. Terrifying experience associated with the *mysterium tremendum* as an epiphanic moment could be converted mentally into the *mysterium fascinans*, or the glass being 'half full, not 'half empty'. This is a spiritual event, or a means to ultimate personal transformation. She writes,

> I was very lucky on this particular day because the sun was shining, and as the next huge wave rolled up behind the boat blocking out the sun, the sun shone through the top of it and the colours of the sunlight refracting through the water were just magnificent. I immediately thought that not many people would get to see a sight like it from that angle and how beautiful the waves were. So, after that, the bigger the waves got the more beautiful they became, and that's when I realised you definitely **can** change your thoughts if you put enough practice and conviction into it.[41]

At the end of the day, Cottee's lesson is one of inner growth, or an inner reframing of self-worth as a moral being above all else. The human virtue of "wisdom" manifests in her character. Such insight is fashioned by the inchoate sea and wind and all of the chthonic forces at work in combination with them:

> . . . there are not enough years of life given to any of us to accomplish all of our dreams and hopes. Some people battle all their lives to get somewhere or do something, against insur-mountable odds, only to end their existence as they started out—frustrated and incomplete. Happiness and pleasure at all times with whatever we do in life, whilst working towards a goal or actually achieving it, should be

---

40.   *Ibid,* 77.
41.   *Ibid.*

the prime objective. That's not to say we should be greedy with our time and spend it on ourselves and our projects, becoming single-minded, selfish bores (which I felt I was sometimes, in the months before leaving on the trip, nearly destroying some precious friendships in the process).[42]

Lesson learned, Kay Cottee was on her way home a changed woman, perhaps with a maturity that would allow her to go home but never again as she first imagined she would, only to fall again into dependency on others for her self-esteem. She became free from all that.

* * *

So, sailors may hope to sail *wisely*. Doing so catapults them into always facing life itself in the face of death itself. Presented are occasions for reflection on just what they understand themselves to be as human beings first, competent yachtsmen second. Being in peril at sea could well turn into damnation and demise, but also it could be redemptive, or a personal process of 'getting life into proper perspective'. While astronauts could take 'one step for a man and one giant leap for mankind', a sailor at sea is no less a voyager stepping ahead on behalf of their individual lives and also for the entire human species.[43] Especially for the single-handed sailor, when the chips are down and peril is imminent, doing things to survive is critical. However, they would be regressive as people were they to respond only in a reactionary manner without also being morally present at such times, when little more can be done to survive. Important questions arise. Is a sailor able to find an 'inner calm' amidst calamitous circumstances and learn to be totally 'present' within such a personal storm? Being who they may become as peril is faced may be more important than survival itself. Sometimes doing nothing saves the day, for example, not abandoning a dismasted yacht that remains afloat. Are they reactionary? Do they panic or despair when things break down? Or does a paradox of 'action through inaction' appear? Is being present to witness such circumstances a deliberate

---

42. Kay Cottee, *First Lady: A History-Making Solo Voyage Around the World* (Sydney: Pan Books, 1990), 159–160.

43. See Erikson; Jonas.

stance, rather than automatically and without consideration trying to do more when little more can realistically be done? To be present is to insert human vitality into perilous circumstances, and that is about all that is called for when nothing else can be done. In general, the study of sport and its relationship to developing spiritual insight and overall moral resilience ('character') remains important to the maturing consciousness or global human spirit. For example, yachting worldwide can be more than simply knowing how to sail from 'Point A' to 'Point B' and theory about what to do in emergencies. Like other sports, yachting also can facilitate knowing who people are as human beings in the universe, with the sea as a microcosm of nature's indifference, impartiality and caprice in regard to human will.

The human face of the sport is what makes yachting so compelling. In the end, it could be said that the sport of yachting is drama writ large, a combination of comedy and tragedy all in one. Only around the edges of the drama is the technology of yachts and their equipment a topic worth consideration. The comic aspect of the sport would certainly include the often obscenely exorbitant financial costs for state-of-the-art boats, equipment and, in highly competitive racing, professional crews. For the average weekend sailing aspirant, the costs of marina berths, annual haul-outs, regular anti-fouling of the boat's hull and the not infrequent need for repairs is laughable to outside observers. Some standard jokes in this regard go like this: 'Yachting is like standing in a cold shower and tearing up $100 bills' or 'like throwing money into a great hole in the water;' and 'There are two wonderful days in yachting—the one when you buy the boat and then the day when the boat is finally sold.' Indeed, even committed yachting people often wonder why in the world they ever got into sailing in the first place, and what keeps them 'hanging in there'. The comic irony of yachting escapes no one, and it always elicits a chuckle.

The tragic dimension of the human drama of yachting takes in all of the existential peril that is faced both by competitive racing and leisurely cruising sailors. Peril is taken on board and reckoned with over the course of time and miles offshore on the high seas far from effective immediate assistance. For average sailors the standard advice is, 'Log on with the Coast Guard before setting out'. No search and rescue procedures will be put in place if a yacht calls the Coast Guard on the radio upon returning to the marina to 'log off,' indicating that a safe and sound return from a sailing venture. Weekend sailing is hardly high drama, though it can become so. However, the same cannot be said for much longer passages. For offshore sailors, tragedies can be woven out of the jagged separations of leaving family and friends behind, psychological oscillations between profound solitude and unsettling hallucinations inhabited by companions of varying sorts, real anxieties about the boat striking whales or shipping containers that have fallen off ships and float just below the surface of the ocean, being unable to control the yacht in wind and waves, worry about one's mental health and whether a voyage will succeed. Whether the human drama of going to the sea in a yacht is more or less comic or tragic must be discerned case by case from reports of sailors themselves. Only afterwards do the meanings of their voyages dawn on most sailors. Most single-handed circumnavigators of the globe attest to having been profoundly changed by what they did and all that happened to them at sea. If yachting is drama write large, combining comedy and tragedy all at once, then a naïve or shortsighted reliance on the technology of yachting can make voyaging into a fool's paradise.

Perhaps it goes back to the kind of worldview that one assumes, and whether it is like the pre-modern earth-centred vision of Ptolemy or the modern 'cosmic' outlook of Copernicus and moon-based astronauts. The pre-modern worldview always implied that when human beings found themselves in difficulties, then appeals could be put to higher powers or 'God' for divine help. Christianity (and Islam among world religions) represents such a clarion call most. In pre-Christian ancient Greek drama, such appeals were represented on stage by a simple technical device called a *deus ex machina*, or 'god from a machine'. Attached to the set on which a dramatic performance would be staged was a small crane. The crane was used to lower props as needed into scenes of the play being acted out below. Included among various props were 'gods'. They represented the chief divine and semi-divine players of Greek mythology. Representations of Zeus, Prometheus, and Demeter and so on could be attached to the *deus ex machina* and lowered into dramatic performances, and this was done usually at moments of heightened comic or tragic feeling in the audience. The 'gods' could always be relied on to 'save the day' for mere mortals or condemn them to tragic fates. The stage-bound mortals always happened to find themselves in difficulties that evoked crying and tears of sorrow as well as peals of laughter and joy from onlookers. The result was a *catharsis*, or sense of emotional release and insight into the drama of being human across the crowded amphitheatre.

The chief question this raises is, will single-handed circumnavigating sailors (and others) persist in hoping that something like a *deus ex machina* will help them sort out their perilous human dramas at sea? In other words, how might sailors with an otherwise 'blind faith' in technical self-reliance learn to abandon hope that such modern 'gods' will appear and be effective when they think they are most needed? And so sailors play their parts on the dramatic stage of the sea. Some soar to heights of technical skill thinking nothing of it, until things begin falling apart and nothing goes exactly according to plan, and when it would be comical if that was all there was to it. Do the 'wheels fall off' the *deus ex machina* of technical self-reliance? Other sea-bound actors venture bravely into the whirlpool of such comedy, where they enter into a maelstrom of desperation that leads to tragedy, perhaps even to their deaths. These sailors are forced to face themselves without "gods" of heaven above or technology below, teetering on a watery abyss all by themselves. If, somehow, the *deus ex machina* of technical self-reliance can be repaired, if the 'wheels' can be put back on, then they can continue to believe that survival may become much more possible. However, a general sense of futility persists in all of it. Such is the existential nature of the human drama at hand for most single-handed sailors, and perhaps for other sporting people.

A critically important point must be noted. It is not the technological device of the 'god machine' itself that is so important. The most important thing is the human end served by the *deus ex machina*, whatever form that technological device may take in critical moments on the ocean. (Does the radio suddenly work again? Does rain replenish empty water tanks? Do flooded bilges pump dry? Does the chopper locate the damaged yacht? Is a long-missing bottle of brandy finally found?) Between tragedy and comedy, the most important thing that is served by technology (that is, a physical extension of human will) at sea is the human drama played out to a final catharsis by the yachtsman. Such a catharsis is a spiritual operation that transforms the seemingly mirror-like waters of the sea into an impregnable 'Other' in the modern period, neither friend nor foe by dint of its indifference to a person's life. As single-handed sailor and author, Jonathan Raban puts it,

> In a secular world, it is this sacral quality of the sea that survives most vividly in poetry of our own time. The sea lies on the far margin of society, and it is—as nothing else is—serious and deep. The last line of Derek Walcott's epic narrative poem, *Omeros*, has Achilles (a West Indian fisherman who, in Alcott's poem as in Homer's *Iliad*, is the prototype of a busy, mortal man) walking away from the end of the story: When he left the beach the sea was still going on.[44]

The sea is made to reflect not only its impartial and perilous nature, but also all that the sailors have witnessed of themselves out there unaided and mirrored by the sea, either liking or worrying about what they observe about themselves. Bearing such witness to oneself pressed into personal peril in sport is a stepping-stone to spiritual insight. That sort of insight leads to a life in which doing nothing may often be the most effective action to take and represent a zenith of human value. This is especially so when the ever-veiled cosmic stakes that underscore human existence are taken into account, terms for living that embrace failure and defeat and, nonetheless, make for exhilaration and a revitalisation of life come what may.

---

44. Jonathan Raban, editor, *The Oxford Book of the Sea* (Oxford and New York: Oxford University Press, 1992), 32.

Endnotes

*.   This article reflects a larger research project in which not only autobiographical accounts of sailors' recollections are reviewed. It also relies on personal interviews with some notable Australian single-handed global circumnavigators (for example, Jesse Martin of *Lionheart*, 1998–1999) and shipwrecked sailors of the Sydney to Hobart Yacht Race (for example, John 'Steamer' Stanley ot *Winston Churchill*, 1998).

+.   Perhaps a fourth way in which moral presence dawns in the awareness of single-handed or 'solo' sailors is through experiencing voyages and trials at sea as *Dreams and Nightmares,* but such awareness comes only in glimpses, each with different human lessons to teach, if surviving technically at sea is effective enough. Whereas moral presence as *Technical Finesse, Cosmic Quest* and *Personal Test* are clearly evident in the lives of sailors, 'Dreams and Nightmares' lack clarity. Moral presence as a clear realisation is clouded by shadows of profound and ongoing uncertainty; it does not build up continuities of significant human themes that go to coherent self-understandings, being only partial in nature. One is led to wonder whether sailors actually are fully 'awake' to what is at stake, or whether their innocence and/or lack of technical skill at sea together represent a 'slumber' or somnolence of a sort. Eventually, these sorts of sailors 'wake up' to what they have done, but this occurs usually well after the fact of their voyages. The lucky ones, like seventeen-year-old Australian Jesse Martin, eventually fulfil their dream, though the gravity of undertaking a solo circumnavigation around the globe floated on his naïveté and lots of backing from sponsors, family and friends. Martin was often pleasantly overcome by a vague sense of higher purpose that undergirded his solo circumnavigation from Melbourne from the end of 1998 and through most of 1999, but the nature of that purpose remained elusive. (See Jesse Martin, *Lionheart: A Journey of the Human Spirit,*Crows Nest, New South Wales: Allen & Unwin, 2001.) Unlucky somnolent sailors, like Tami Ashcraft, seek only an end to their dream-turned-nightmare. Her boyfriend was swept overboard and lost at sea while they were making a yacht delivery from Tahiti to San Diego, California. Ashcraft knew very little about sailing. Her terror was stayed only by an 'inner voice,' a sign of being on the verge of imminent personal disintegration and psychosis, though she managed to survive in the end and reach Hawaii. Also naïve, such unlucky sailors are thrown into treacherous circumstances against their will, and must somehow try to maintain inner strength to survive. (See Tami Oldham Ashcraft, *Red Sky in Mourning: The True Story of a Woman's Courage and Survival at Sea*, London: Simon & Schuster, 2002.)

Chapter Six

The Call Of The Game

Chris Gardiner

You are at the football (and let me immediately declare a bias: by football, I mean the world game, the beautiful game). For the last ten minutes the game has been very exciting. Two spectators behind you are discussing the game, as one of the players is down and there is an injury stoppage.

'Ya know, if it wasn't for the rules, we wouldn't be enjoying this game as much as we are', says one. 'You're right', says the other, 'and can you imagine what a disaster this would be without a referee – lucky he's here'.

Not a very likely exchange?

Millions of people every week play or watch football, and they do so with passion. Most will be able to recall moments in games they played or have watched that made them oblivious to all other reality. Some of those experiences remain seared into their memories, indeed in some cases, into their identities. Most, however, do not realise that the game 'experience' is manufactured, the result of a human artefact crafted, in its essential details, by a committee, in England in the mid-nineteenth century. At the heart of the experience is a set of rules—the hallowed 'Laws of the Game'—and crucial to most serious occasions of game play is the rule keeper—the referee. Unfortunately, most will only ever realise these truths in moments of frustration and anger, when the referee has made a mistake or 'had a bad game', and they are resenting the fact that the experience they had hoped for in attending the game has been denied them 'because he just doesn't know the rules'.

I want to spend some time reflecting on how humans experience and build value through the rule-based activities called games, reflect on how important referees are to experiencing the value we seek, and think about the virtues that might be articulated to underpin the practice and service of the referee. I want to do so because, like so many others, football matters to me—I love the game, it adds to my identity, it helps me explain what it means to be human—to my children, to my friends, to my community.

My basic point will be: many of us respond to the 'call of the game', but whether we actually enjoy the resulting experience depends on the referee's actual call of the game, and that, therefore, we should do more to ensure that that call is consistently excellent.

Games and being human

We humans regulate our environment and relationships to obtain what we desire and that which we value. When we have a positive experience, when we realise the value of an object or experience, we work to structure relationships and interactions to recreate the experience, or to preserve and promote the valued object or experience, or indeed to promote a value expressed as a concept and norm. Three of the things humans experience positively are the physical use of their bodies, achievement, and social recognition for achievement. We simply enjoy running fast, for example; we enjoy throwing objects, especially if we do it successfully towards a target; we enjoy solving problems; and most of all we enjoy being validated by recognition and status obtained through these sometimes simple achievements—'good girl, you run so fast'.

We humans are game players, not least because the game enables physical and mental expression and achievement.[1] A mix of bio-psycho-social prompts and rewards underpin what I would describe as the 'call of the game'. We experience the hormonal and chemical thrills of achievement in the games we create, especially when it is an achievement against the odds or with heightened risk. We also experience the status benefits of being recognised as excelling in the game or as being the champion over others (especially if the recognition is driven

---

1.   For an introduction to thinking about humans and play see K Blanchard, *The Anthropology of Sport: An Introduction* (London: Bergin & Garvey, 1995), P Smith, editor, *Play In Animals and Humans* (Oxford: Basil Blackwell, 1984), J Huizinga, *Homo Ludens: A Study of the Play Element in Culture* (Boston: Beacon Press, 1950), and R Callois, *Man, Play & Games* (New York: Free Press, 1961), B Suits, What is a Game?' in *Philosophy of Science*, 34 (June 1967): 148–56; B Heinrich, *Why We Run: A Natural History* (New York: Ecco, 2001).

by vicarious identification with a victory over another community or group). As children, we run, and dance, and weave, and wrestle, and throw objects, and play tricks, and experiment with tunes, and mimic adults in role playing. Especially where our circumstances allow 'free time' away from the necessities of subsistence and production, as adults and communities we create opportunities, facilities and competitions to recreate these early childhood experiences of play, and institutionalise them as 'sports'.

Games take various forms, depending on the artificial test constructed by the rules of each game. The aim is always some kind of physical and/ or psychological/mental challenge—to run a limited distance within a period of time, to throw an object a certain distance, to solve a problem of strategy. Variables are manipulated to heighten risk or pose barriers or make comparisons—you not only run the distance, you run against another person or against the time you set last time. You not only throw the object a distance, you change the weight of the object. You not only create an artificial game area with rules that mimic battles (chess), you also limit the way certain instruments in the game can be moved, and place a time limit on how long a decision can take for a particular movement. The target or goal is given a maximum height or width, a person or persons are placed to defend it, the freedom of movement in the area in front of the goal is limited, and, again, a time limit is set.

Central to most games is the contest against these barriers—we humans, it seems, naturally 'benchmark' ourselves. We play a game against another person or team, not just as a barrier to be overcome, but so as to know, by comparison, how clever, how excellent we really are.

In regulating our environment and relationships, we come to see one of the other aspects of what it means to be human—we create rules, we expect of each other reasons for breaking rules, and we seek structures to enforce rules and sanction breaches. One of our first experiences of rule making, rule following and rule enforcement, is in game playing. And in the reality of game playing, if most participants are to enjoy the game, we have to know the rules. Indeed for the game to continue, outside the dominance of a psychopath (in which case, it is his game experience alone), the participants must not only know the rules but accept them—they must 'play by the rules'. We come to learn something about ourselves, as a result, when confronted by the 'cheat'—humans are offended by unfair dealings, withdrawing from the exchange, or excluding the cheat from our game, or taking time to punish the cheat.

Games are pleasurable and validating experiences and they come to matter to us, and sports based institutions characterise our societies as a result. But, importantly, we come to realise that we can learn what it means to be human in these games – recognising both our basic nature and our potential for transcendence of that nature in 'the way the game is played'. As a result, adults use games to teach children values and to reinforce social moralities around commitment, loyalty, fairness, courage and resilience.[2] And into and around our games we weave stories, because we humans are story tellers—we find pleasure in recounting experiences, and we find story telling an important way of providing concrete mental images and memories of the morality we wish our children and selves to honour.[3]

Games and referees

Games that become socially significant usually require referees. The need for a game arbiter, umpire or referee develops in games for three reasons. The first and second are closely linked to the need for and nature of rules in the first place, and here I draw on the work of Mihaly Csikszentmihalyi.[4] Csikszentmihalyi has researched what he calls the 'phenomenology of enjoyment' and the 'experience of flow':

> the phenomenology of enjoyment has eight major components. When people reflect on how it feels when their experience is most positive, they mention at least one, and often all, of the following. First, the experience usually occurs when we confront tasks we have a chance of completing. Second, we must be able to concentrate on what we are doing. Third and fourth, the concentration is usually possible because the task undertaken has clear

2.   See for example G Selleck, *Raising a Good Sport in an In-Your-Face-World* (New York: Contemporary, 2002).

3.   See, for example, V Fortanescu *Life Lessons from Soccer* (New York: Simon & Schuster, 2001).

4.   M Csikszentmihalyi, *Flow: The Psychology of Optimal Experience* (New York: Harper Perennial, 1991).

goals and provides immediate feedback. Fifth, one acts
with a deep but effortless involvement that removes from
awareness the worries and frustrations of everyday life.
Sixth, enjoyable experiences allow people to exercise a
sense of control over their actions. Seventh, concern for the
self disappears, yet paradoxically the sense of self emerges
stronger after the flow experience is over. Finally, the sense
of duration of time is altered; hours pass by in minutes, and
minutes can stretch out to seem like hours. The combination
of all these elements causes a sense of deep enjoyment that
is so rewarding people feel that expending a great deal of
energy is worthwhile simply to be able to feel it.[5]

Csikszentmihalyi identifies the steps involved in creating the
experience of flow: you must set an overall goal and as many sub-goals
as are realistically feasible; find ways of measuring progress in terms
of these goals; keep concentrating and making finer distinctions in the
challenges involved; develop skills necessary to interact and control the
opportunities; and you must keep raising the stakes.

Games and sport are ways to create and recreate flow experiences,
and Csikszentmihalyi and others have explored the relevance of the
concept of flow for play, sport and coaches.[6] The important point to note
is that the nature and extent of the rules for a game influence the quality
of the experience. One of the key aspects of flow is not only that the rules
must set clear and attainable goals and allow for initiative, but that they
also work best when they are not the focus of the participant's conscious
thought processes. How is this achieved in a contest of physical contact
and speed and whose outcome has great meaning for the participants?
Well, one of the ways a referee assists the participants to enjoy a game
is by taking away the responsibility for interpreting and enforcing
the rules of the game – the players need to have 'deep but effortless
concentration' on what they are doing, a process assisted by leaving rule
policing to someone else.

5.   *Ibid*, 49.
6.   M Csikszentmihalyi, and S Bennett, 'An Exploratory Model of Play', in *American
     Anthropologist*, 73 (1971): 45–58, and S Jackson, and M Csikszentmihalyi, *Flow in
     Sports* (Champaign: Human Kinetics, 1999).

A second reason a referee becomes necessary is that, for flow to be experienced, the rules must not be complicated, must allow for some freedom and creativity, and must provide for the game to be played with as little interruption and distraction as possible—the play and game flow, in the sense of momentum, becomes important to the individual experience of flow. Good rules allow for freedom and momentum, but where the outcome of the game has social significance, it falls to someone—the referee—to assess whether the freedom sought by a player in any particular instance of play is consistent with the rules of the game, or gives one player or team an advantage. Examples in football include interpretation of the current wording of the Law regarding 'careless, reckless or excessive' play, or the definition of 'foul' or 'dangerous' play, or whether a player's action or words are 'offensive, insulting, or abusive', or whether a player's position is offside by virtue of him interfering with play or gaining an advantage.[7] If the game is to flow, someone must make these decisions, quickly and without challenge, to allow the game to be more than a series of disputes interspersed with play.

Closely linked to the second reason is the third: a referee is needed in serious games of contest to ensure fairness—one of the fundamental values to humans, and central both to the enjoyment of a game and to the social legitimacy of the outcome. The more at stake in a game, the greater the need for an impartial person to arbitrate on those instances where action may be claimed to be outside the rules and to someone's unfair advantage. The faster and more physically intense the game, the more important that someone not invested in the outcome make decisions regarding instances of alleged rule infringement. As an example, consider in a football game making the call during an attacking move as to whether the 'whole of the ball' crossed the sideline or not.

---

7.   FIFA Laws of the Game 2007/2008 (http://www.fifa.com/mm/document/ affederation/federation/laws_of_the_game_0708_10565.pdf accessed 11 November 2007).

Football and the football referee

Football embodies much of the purpose and meaning of game playing I have been discussing above.[8] Its roots can be traced to England in the later Middle Ages, where communities (indeed, in some cases, whole communities!) would engage in intra and inter-communal contests that involved one community or its representatives keeping a ball from the other community side, and delivering it to a designated goal location. These popular events evolved to become formalised contests within the educational institutions of these communities, where their potential became apparent as instruments of character and identity formation.

One of the problems that emerged in England as football itself began to take form, was that when schools moved to test themselves against each other (a vicarious contest waged through their teams), they had difficulty agreeing on the rules of the contest – we can assume that it served no-one, in terms of arguments about the status of the winner, if the loser could simply point to the possibility that the team had played by different rules, and that under *their* rules, the result would have been different! Football, as the world has played the game for nearly 150 years, was 'created' through a committee meeting in London in 1863, by a group of men who wanted to make sure that not only could they play a game of football against each other, but be certain that the result had legitimacy. There would be a winner or loser or no result, and be no argument as to why that was so (although, the rules continued to evolve for decades).

Now the formalisation of the rules of football represented, I think, two different intentions. The first, as in all games, was to set the artificial barriers that would determine the nature and heighten the experience of achievement—the goal being scored by a small object kicked (not handled) into a small area against the efforts of goal area defenders. The second, however, was to ensure that there would be certainty about who had won a particular game or series of games. The game being played was to be both about the experience of scoring goals, and the

---

8. For an introduction to the history of football, see J Walvin, *The People's Game: The History of Football Revisited* (London: Mainstream Publishing, 1994), C Leatherdale, editor, *The Book of Football* (Essex: Desert Island, 1997), D Russell, *Football and the English* (Preston: Carnegie, 1997).

experience of scoring more goals than a competitor/opponent when both competitors had the *same* opportunities. One point of any contest-based game is to be able to claim victory over the competitor/opponent, without that claim itself being contested.

Whilst agreeing the basic rules was important, it came to be clear that one other significant game element needed to be included—an impartial arbiter who could rule in the heat of the contest as to whether the rules were being followed. The role of the referee evolved from the responsibilities of captains to determine contested game incidents, to the appointment by each side of 'neutral' umpires at each end of the field, to the appointment of a third umpire or referee with ultimate decision powers.[9] As the game developed in the late 1800s, and with ongoing rule refinement, the role of the referee grew significantly. With standard rules, more events using those rules, greater social meaning emerging for game outcomes as reflected in the creation of inter-club and inter-country competitions and trophies, greater control of the game was given to the referee. This included keeping time, penalising players, and moving from interpreting and ruling on alleged rule breaches brought to his attention by an 'appeal' (as in cricket), to identifying and penalising infringements himself. By 1893 a separate Referees' Association had been formed, to better prepare, protect and regulate referees themselves.

Today, the referee carries responsibilities extending from whether parents believe their child has been safe in a game and learnt about fairness and sportsmanship, to whether an international event invested with national pride and worth hundreds of millions in gambling and sponsorship is the subject of controversy as to who actually won. And whether it is the reluctance to actually run the local weekend game because there are not enough referees, or the frustration that officiating is below standard and 'we need better referees at this level,' most players and supporters deep down, I think, understand that referees are central to the quality of the game and sport.

We play and create games for physical and mental self-expression and achievement. We value those experiences so much, we create institutional forms of the games we play, and invest in those institutions significant physical and emotional resources. Football is the classic, global example.

---

9. Little appears to have been written about the history of the referee. I draw on G Thomson, *The Man In Black: A History of the Football Referee* (London: Prion, 1998).

Now when you think about the role of the referee, it can be described as follows:

1. The referee is given the power and privilege to control a highly valued social activity, and to make decisions in particular instances on behalf of the broader institution and community and the immediate parties involved, given his status as a referee;

2. An individual must master a defined body of knowledge and practice to for the privilege of being appointed as a referee;

3. An individual is admitted to the ranks of referees only by being assessed by other referees, through formal testing of his/her knowledge and practice, and retains his/her place based on ongoing judgement by other officials against the dual criteria of knowledge and effective application in his/her practice.

By some definitions, the description above puts referees into the category of a profession.[10] I will return to what I see as the implications of this observation shortly. But by another set of definitions—those presented by Alasdair MacIntyre[11]—I think refereeing can be seen as a 'practice', with its own internal 'goods' and a related set of 'virtues'. In this view, refereeing has a relationship to football similar to the relationship of judges to the law (further strengthening the idea of refereeing as a profession).

MacIntyre describes a practice as:

> any coherent and complex form of socially established cooperative human activity through which the goods internal to that form of activity are realized in the course of trying to achieve those standards of excellence which

10. For discussions on professions and professionalization, see AD Abbott, *The System of Professions: An Essay on the Division of Expert Labour* (Chicago: University of Chicago Press, 1988), E Friedson, *Professionalism Reborn: Theory, Prophecy & Policy* (Chicago: University of Chicago, 1994), and M Larson, *The Rise of Professionalism: A Sociological Analysis* (Malden: Blackwell, 2001).
11. A MacIntyre, *After Virtue: A Study in Moral Theory* (London: Duckworth, 1987).

> are appropriate to, and partially definitive of, that form
> of activity, with the result that human powers to achieve
> excellence, and human conceptions of the ends and goods
> involved, are systematically extended.[12]

Now the goods internal to the practice of the referee are to be experienced by the players and spectators: game flow, an uncontested result, and the meaning of the game for both participants and spectators *after* the game (which must be positive, but could be focused on such aspects as the great goals scored, to the efforts of the team despite the loss, and for which the referee is only indirectly responsible). The standards of excellence in this practice relate to the quality of the decisions the referee makes (including the numerous decisions not to intervene and break the flow of the game), and to the prior expertise and fitness levels that assist the referee to make those decisions. MacIntyre links the idea of virtues to this concept of a practice, describing a virtue as

> an acquired human quality the possession and exercise
> of which tends to enable us to achieve those goods which
> are internal to practices and the lack of which effectively
> prevents us from achieving any such goods.[13]

Consistent with this view, I want to suggest that the virtues in refereeing would be impartial judgement, physical fitness, mastery of a body of knowledge, and self-control and resilience on the field of play.

Normally, a profession will have an articulated set of values and ethics, a code by which it and the community judge its actions. The code will nurture self-understanding and identity. It will contribute towards the strengthening of the profession itself.[14] When asked to work with a group of referees to develop such a code, I discovered, surprisingly, that whilst codes had been developed for players, officials and spectators, codes for referees had been slow to emerge. So based on a previous code developed by FIFA for players, I develop the following Code. It

---

12.   *Ibid*, 187.
13.   *Ibid*, 191.
14.   For a discussion on codes of conduct, see D Grace, and S Cohen, *Business Ethics: Australian Problems and Cases* (Melbourne: Oxford University Press, 1996).

represents a philosophy, a set of virtues, and a benchmark against which behaviour and performance could be assessed by referees in determining the fitness of a person to be called a referee.

1. **Help the game and the players be all they can be**

   Soccer is about the players enjoying the game. It is about the players' contest, against themselves, and, as a team, against others. It is about the spectators being entertained by, and taking pride in, the skill and character displayed on the field. It has its own logic, flow and spirit. The referee should not seek to shape a game, or to determine an outcome. The referee's role and responsibility is to help the game and players be all they can be, by giving of their best in each and every game, and by ensuring that the game is played according to the Laws of the Game.

2. **Know and understand the laws of the game**

   The logic and spirit of the game of soccer is expressed in, and given life by, the laws of the game. A referee must not just know the laws. A referee must understand the laws, deeply. A referee should be able to recount the details of the laws. A referee should also be able to apply and interpret the laws on the field. A referee should seek game experience, and advice and instruction from senior referees, to grow in this knowledge. They should attend development and up-date programs. And a person can only become a referee and remain a referee if he or she has passed and continues to pass formal assessment by other referees of his or her understanding of the laws.

3. **Know, master and improve yourself**

   Each of us has strengths and weaknesses. Referees should know their own individual temperament and personality. They should know their fitness level and their capacity for judgement on the field. They should take pride in their strengths and master their weaknesses. They should be willing to admit mistakes. They should accept the guidance of their colleagues when it is expressed in assessments and gradings. They should seek, if they are to be active referees, to use this self-knowledge and the counsel of their colleagues to continually improve their performance as referees. They should be known for their honesty and integrity.

4. **Make decisions fairly and consistently**
    Referees make hundreds of decisions in each game. Many flows of play and actions by players will call for an interpretation of the situation in terms of the Laws of the Game. Referees are expected to decide fairly, by only taking into consideration the facts of the situation and the laws as they apply to that situation. Referees are expected to interpret and apply the laws, to situations, and in regard to players, consistently. Consistency requires not just an understanding of the laws but critical thinking about what you are deciding from one moment to the next and throughout the entire game. And at no time should the origin or background of the players or the previous history of the team or club be a consideration.

5. **Be courageous in protecting the safety and dignity of players**
    Soccer is a game that can involve physical contact and high emotion. A referee must ensure that equipment, individual behaviour, the mood of the game, or the conditions of the ground do not place the safety of players at risk. The referee must also safeguard the dignity of players in terms of abusive, offensive or insulting language or behaviour. Where the safety or dignity of players is threatened, the referee must take control of the game by enforcing the laws, without regard to criticism or the reaction of players, spectators or officials.

6. **Respect the players, parents, spectators and officials at the game**
    Always treat players, and the parents, spectators and officials

who support them, with the greatest respect. Never talk down to or belittle anyone at a game. Always be courteous. Refrain from arguing about decisions and from responding to abuse or criticism. Remember that discretion is the better part of valour, which means seeking to avoid a confrontation. Your interaction with the players, parents, spectators and officials reflects on you, other referees and the game itself.

7. **Honour and support other referees**

   Always respect, remain loyal to and support other referees. Work as a team when appointed to the same game and seek to encourage each other during and after the game. Do not publicly question or criticise another referee's decision or performance. This loyalty, respect and support should be shown whether you are refereeing, playing, coaching or a spectator or official. Rather, if you have a difference of opinion or can provide constructive criticism, do so in person, privately, or through the appropriate referee association processes.

8. **Discharge your field and administrative duties professionally**

   Always conduct yourself professionally. Allocate sufficient time to arrive well before a game to check the field, player equipment and game paperwork. Take pride in your appearance before, during and after the game. Make every effort to provide accurate and complete game reports and to ensure that these reach the appropriate official by the necessary post-game deadlines.

9. **Promote refereeing**

   Soccer needs referees. Refereeing needs organizations to assess, appoint and develop referees, and to contribute to the on-going development of the game at local, national and international levels. Actively participate in your association, support its decisions and support its development. Take every opportunity to encourage others to contribute to the game by becoming referees.

10. Promote soccer, the laws of the game and FIFA's code of conduct

As the FIFA Code of Conduct affirms, Soccer is the world's greatest game. Take every opportunity to promote the game. Take every opportunity to educate its supporters in the Laws of the Game. Take every opportunity to promote the FIFA Code of Conduct. And as that Code says, help others to have as much fun from Soccer as you do.

Is football, and refereeing, that important?

Michael Novak, the great Catholic philosopher, starts his reflections on sport with the statement: 'Sport is, somehow, a religion. You either see or you don't see what the excitement is'.[15] He goes on, talking about American football in his case:

> The basic reality of all human life is play, games, sport; these are the realities from which the basic metaphors for all that is important in the rest of life are drawn. Work, politics, and history are the illusory, misleading, false world. *Being, beauty, truth, excellence, transcendence* – these words, grown in the soil of play, wither in the sand of work. Art, prayer, worship, love, civilization: these thrive in the field of play. Play belongs to the Kingdom of Ends, work to the Kingdom of Means. Barbarians play in order to work; the civilized work in order to play . . . Football makes conscious to me part of what I am. And what football says about me, and about millions of others like me, is not half as ugly as it is beautiful. Seeing myself reflected in the dance, the agony and the ritual of a heated contest, I am at peace.[16]

---

15. M Novak, *The Joy of Sports: End Zones, Bases, Baskets, Balls and the Consecration of the American Spirit* (New York: Basic Books, 1976), xi.
16. *Ibid*, xii and xv.

Players and spectators in and at a football match have responded to the call of the game—the desire to achieve, the desire to be thrilled by that achievement, the desire to win in a contest against a team equally determined to win. It seems we are made this way. Here's my point, then, about that most valuable of human artefacts and experiences, football – the integrity of the football experience, in the games that matter, depends to a very large extent on the referee's actual call of the game. For something so important to so many of us, having referees live by a code similar to that outlined above would be bring great satisfaction, perhaps even joy, to the millions of humans who see that part of being human means being footballers or football fans.

Contributors

Chris Gardiner is the Chief Executive Officer of the Police & Community Youth Clubs NSW (PCYC), a major non-government provider of sports programs for young people. He is President of Parramatta FC, and was previously an active member of the Nepean District Soccer Referees Association. He has postgraduate qualifications in professional ethics and in international relations.

Dr **Rob Hess** is a Senior Lecturer in sport history with the School of Sport and Exercise Science at Victoria University. He is also the Publications Officer for the Australian Society for Sports History, and the co-author of *A National Game: The History of Australian Rules Football* (Penguin/Viking, 2008).

Associate Professor **Richard Hutch** is a Reader in Religion and Psychological Studies in the School of History, Philosophy, Religion and Classics at the University of Queensland. His research interests include psychology of religion, sport and spirituality, self-narrations and life-writing, and death and dying. He is the author of *Lone Sailors and Spiritual Insights: Cases of Sport and Peril at Sea*, published by the Edwin Mellen Press, 2005.

Rev'd Dr **Victor C Pfitzner** is a Lutheran pastor, now living in retirement. Postgraduate theological studies in Germany, in the early 1960s, were completed with a doctoral dissertation on use of traditional athletic imagery in the letters of St Paul. He served as a parish pastor and university chaplain in Brisbane for several years. In 1968 he became a foundation member of the faculty of Luther Seminary, North Adelaide (now Australian Lutheran College) where he served for nearly forty years as lecturer in New Testament, including nine years as principal.

Rev'd Dr **Gordon Preece** was formerly Executive Director of Urban Seed, Melbourne, editor of Zadok Perspectives, ethical consultant to Christian Super and adjunct lecturer in ethics for Ridley College, Bible College of Victoria, University of Otago and The School of Applied Finance, Macquarie University. He is an ordained Anglican minister and former director of Ridley College Centre for Applied Christian Ethics and Macquarie Christian Studies Institute. He is author/editor of ten books on ethical issues and many articles. He played one season of pitifully paid semi-professional football (soccer) for Pan Hellenic in Sydney, but now confines himself to indoor football and following the perennially disappointing Spurs.

Dr **Synthia Sydnor** is an associate professor of Kinesiology and Community Health at the University of Illinois at Urbana-Champaign, USA. She has been a National Endowment for the Humanities fellow (Periklean Athens); book review editor of the *Journal of Sport History;* an assistant editor of *Journal of Sport and Social Issues,* and past chair of the Sport Sociology Academy of the National Alliance of Health, Physical Education, Recreation and Dance. Her research has appeared in a range of international venues and she is the co-editor/author of the book, *To the Extreme: Alternative Sports, Inside and Out,* that confronts questions about the essences, nature and origins of sport.

CPSIA information can be obtained
at www.ICGtesting.com
Printed in the USA
FFOW02n1950150914
7384FF